# The Queen Of Romance

## The Life And Legacy Of Barbara Cartland

Eliza Morgan Chase

Global East-West. London

Copyright © [2025] by Eliza Morgan Chase.

"What Do You Know About?" A Global East-West Series.

All rights reserved. No part of this book may be reproduced in any manner whatsoever without written permission, except for brief quotations incorporated into critical articles and reviews.

# Contents

1. Introduction 1
   The Romantic Legacy of Barbara Cartland

2. Early Life and Influences 17
   From Birmingham to Society's Spotlight

3. A Tragic Beginning 35
   The Impact of World War I

4. First Steps in Literature 53
   The Making of a Romance Icon

5. The Hallmark of Romance 71
   Crafting the Perfect Historical Love Story

6. Beyond the Pen 89
   Cartland's Influence and Advocacy

7. Pink Perfection 105
   Cultivating an Enchanting Public Persona

8. Royal Connections 121
   Guiding the Princess of Wales

| 9. Wartime Contributions | 141 |
| --- | --- |
| Service, Sacrifice, and Society | |
| 10. Critics vs. Commercial Success | 159 |
| The Dichotomy of Definition | |
| 11. Legacy of Love | 179 |
| Cartland's Continued Relevance | |
| 12. Conclusion | 197 |
| Defining a Genre for Generations | |
| Bibliographic Selection | 215 |

# Introduction

## THE ROMANTIC LEGACY OF BARBARA CARTLAND

## The Enduring Allure of Romance Novels

Romance novels, filled with manifestations of love and its overwhelming emotions, have revolved in our society for centuries, captivating readers from all walks of life. They allow readers to be captivated in far-off worlds where they can enjoy the thrill, struggles, and victories of love alongside their beloved characters. Romance novels provide the much-needed refuge from reality and a foray into the complexities of human love and relationships in the famous "happily ever after" world. It can be said that such novels have been giving solace to readers of all ages by touching their hearts and souls through captivating stories cleverly woven by the authors.

Romance novels shed light on the deepest of human desires and the empty feeling every individual feels in isolation, that is, the longing for intimacy and connection. They reflect the human experience. Their portrayal of different aspects of romance demonstrates the joy that comes with love alongside the challenges, soothing every reader's heart, which is one of the many reasons that romance novels have a special corner in readers' hearts.

Moreover, the romance genre is not a monolith. It is a diverse and inclusive space that accommodates a wide variety of tastes. Whether you're into Historical Romance, Contemporary Romance, Paranormal Romance, or Romantic Suspense, there's a book for you. Each subgenre offers a unique take on love, with storytelling components that capture the attention and interests of readers. This diversity allows romance novels to cater to different cultural, social, and personal contexts, offering a broader selection of ideas for one to ponder.

Furthermore, the unwavering optimism that romance novel readers experience has a profoundly soothing effect on the heart and mind. In a world filled with stressors and unpredictability, romance novels offer a comforting escape. They remind us that love wins in the end, regardless of the odds. This reassurance provides ample reasons to hope, dream, and escape reality, reinforcing the belief in love's power to redeem.

As a result, readers have come to associate the enduring charm of romance novels with their ability to transport one to a world of heightened emotions. These factors work in harmony to create the irresistible and undeniable appeal that these novels possess, underscoring their significance in literature and captivating the interest of readers.

# Barbara Cartland: A Timeless Icon

Barbara Cartland, often hailed as the 'Queen of Romance,' remains a formidable presence in the literary world, her influence transcending time and place. Her nearly century-long career in romantic fiction sets her apart as one of the most remarkable figures in the genre. As an author, socialite, and advocate, she continues to inspire and remains an unparalleled icon.

What separates Cartland from her contemporaries is not the sheer number of her published works but rather the pioneering spirit she embodied in the romance genre. Her extraordinary grasp of human feelings, coupled with her boldness in exploring the intricacies of love, has echoed through many generations, raising her to the status of a symbol of romance literature. Moreover, her prolific output of 700 novels translated into many languages attests to her success and popularity.

In spite of her literary accomplishments, Cartland's public image and societal contributions reinforced her standing as an important cultural personality. Her dignified, regal, and equally philanthropic noteworthy contributions to nurturing emerging writers were some of the many factors that made Cartland a shining pillar of grace. She advocated for numerous charitable causes that went beyond the bounds of her mesmerising fairy tales and indelibly touched the lives of many.

Cartland's innovative writing style, accompanied by her incredible storytelling skills, makes her stand out in the world of romantic fiction. Her ability to blend passion, chivalry, and even love into tales, along with history and strong female characters, made them extremely popular. Her remarkable approach to love stories has greatly surpassed time and will continue influencing countless readers and writers for generations.

Understandably, Cartland's unwavering pursuit of preserving the romantic essence of love and its significance in our lives is the leading reason for her enduring figure. This makes asserting that the legacy Cartland has left behind will always ensure a continual source of inspiration for many who seek comfort in love and the exquisite tales moderated with it.

# The Genesis of Romantic Narrative

An intricate tale of romance, adventure, and chivalry has excited audiences from various cultures throughout the centuries. Following the strands of sophisticated literature, it appears passionate love has been a recurrent motif in human societies for centuries. Love has been an enduring theme throughout literary history, from Homer's 'Iliad' and 'Odyssey' to medieval romances of armour-clad knights. These stories captured idealistic love, astounding acts of valour, and the mixed bag of human feelings, which prepared the foundation for today's romance literature. Strong admiration was at the heart of the chivalric code and courtly love, which reveres respect and adoration towards the subjects of affection. With the progression of societies, romance evolved parallel to the world's social standards and norms. The Renaissance period led to a barrage of sonneteers, playwrights, and prose romantics, who, at great length, detailed the entanglements of amorous liaisons that blended fiercely with tragedy or comedy. In the romance literature timeline, this was the period when profound emotions and self-development became prevalent themes. The form of a novel allowed the authors to freely portray human emotions and to intricately weave relationships. Early romantic novelists, like Jane Austen and the Brontë Sisters, had the unique ability to craft romances seated in social realities and intellect, which was inspirational for countless generations after them. This is best exemplified by Barbara Cartland, who filled her books with love, honour, and virtue themes. Her contribution to the genre was a display of her storytelling brilliance and a testament to the enduring appeal of romance in literature.

## Cultural Impact and Societal Influence

Barbara Cartland's literary contributions have gone far beyond the world of fiction and deeply impacted societal and cultural aspects. Her romantic tales have had a tremendous impact, influencing the concepts of love, relationships, and even chivalry for countless readers. Cartland's construction of superbly romanticised worlds did not only make her emerge as a cultural icon; rather, her influence surged far beyond literature.

The novels of Cartland portrayed an unrealistic yet extraordinarily sought-after vision of romance that many wished to attain. Her ingenious ability to weave tales of love and commitment captured the hearts of many readers across the globe, and the reputation of love skyrocketed in popular culture because of her. In her works, we see the portrayal of love as an indomitable force that unites people, which, for the most part, is an extremely positive notion. However, these scenarios were often fictitious and thus are stripes contrary to the norms and conventions of society.

Cartland's works had a twofold impact on society. They also brought back certain forgotten norms and values. Her works have been known to present a glorified narrative celebrating etiquette, courtship, and moral candour. They might be regarded as fictitious, but in a way, such claims have helped preserve some culture, which is now embedded in the minds of the people who read her works.

In addition to entertainment, Cartland's effect was felt when her writings offered students hope during hard times, granting them solace and escape during difficult periods in society. Her writings perpetuated optimism and undying belief in love and provided sanctuary for countless readers, shaping their responses towards the real world.

Cartland's influence towards romance novels was also the precursor of changes in the societal perspective on love and courtship – allure, romance, and femininity – toward the favourable. While incredibly problematic, her novels attempted to push boundaries and sparked conversations about gender, women's independence, and going beyond just relationships for debates within society.

The cultural and societal impact of Cartland's work showcases her ability to capture people's imagination when detailing romances. Her work shaped gender expectations and values, making it possible for societies, cultures, and literature to undergo shifts and adapt to modern norms and values that are still apparent today.

## Romance: A Literary Phenomenon

In past centuries, literature has exhibited romance as one of its primary phenomena at the global level of genre operations. Romance is a fiction category based on love, where characters form affectionate bonds that capture human emotion. Romance novels have evolved from courtly medieval romances to contemporary tales of passion and desire catered to various audiences. Barbara Cartland is a prolific writer of romantic novels who laid the foundations for the enduring appeal of romantic storytelling with her extensive output and dedication to the genre. The thematic richness encompassed in romances, which stems from universally accepted truths about human nature, facilitates deeply resonant personal growth alongside complex interpersonal narratives that invite the reader into the world presented on the pages. Romance authors can entertain readers and evoke profound reflection as skilled character development with emotive prose evokes empathy through understanding.

The immense popularity of romance literature is owed to its unique ability to provoke an array of feelings, from joy to pain, while simultaneously cultivating trust in the everlasting nature of love. Whether set in times far-off or in the present, romance novels offer thoroughly captivating escapism by whisking readers to places where love and attraction are abundant.

The financial prosperity of romance novels highlights their importance as a category in literature, captivating a loyal audience and proving their lasting acceptance. As romance can operate without bound as a social construct, it furthers attempts to break barriers and reinforces its position in the literary world. The unfiltered emotions and multidimensional celebration of love invite us to the sublime world of romance literature.

# A Glimpse into Her Prolific Output

Barbara Cartland's literary legacy depicts such scope of productivity and output. Over seven decades, Cartland seemed to have had a preposterous number of romance novels under her name, which seemingly never ceased to charm readers worldwide. This resulted from her extraordinary discipline towards her work, which saw her producing at least 23 books annually, frequently finishing a book in 10 days. This astounding output, which exceeds 700 published works, demonstrates her unparalleled work ethic and deep-rooted passion for storytelling.

What sets Cartland apart is not just the sheer number of her novels, but the diversity of her narratives. Her stories traverse multiple historical eras and geographies, from medieval Europe to Regency England. Each tale, while rooted in love and deep affection, is a testament to her belief in the triumph of good over evil. Cartland's novels are not just gripping stories with richly developed characters, but they also redefine the romance genre with their unique narrative style.

Cartland's ability to connect with her audience on an intimate emotional level sets her apart from her contemporaries. Her stories evoke tender emotions and romantic fantasies in readers, providing a much-needed escape from the world. By deeply understanding human feelings and hopes, she crafts timeless stories that continue to resonate with readers, even today.

Cartland's wide-ranging romance novels, which include historical sagas, exotic adventures, and stories with elements of fairy tales, have garnered her considerable attention. Her diverse writing caters to a wide audience, making her immensely popular among different types of readers. Her unique approach of intertwining social concerns with romance showcases her depth of thinking and elevates her work beyond mere entertainment, establishing her as an important literary figure.

In summary, Barbara Cartland's career showcases a remarkable feat of her creativity, work ethic, and commitment to bringing joy and escapism to her readers. Her unparalleled body of work continues to inspire and delight a myriad of romance readers all over the world, cementing her status as a perennial figure in the history of romantic works.

## Critiques and Contributions to the Genre

Catherine Cookson's books are an enduring feature of contemporary popular folk culture in England, and they stand out among other folk literary works of the 20th century.

Spend any time online, 20 minutes or 20 years, and there's a high chance you've encountered a Cookson book. The sheer volume of titles available, not to mention the author's phenomenal popularity, means there is always a plethora of Cookson works waiting to be uncovered, regardless of location. These folk novels are well-known and cherished works of literature that are world-famous for their clever blend of captivating stories and relatable themes. Readers of all ages pick up these deceptively simple yet highly complex novels with great fascination. Cookson is an author unlike any other, with a truly distinctive and one-of-a-kind style that leaves everyone utterly spellbound.

Writing under a pseudonym and living an utterly inconspicuous life, Catherine was determined to become a great writer. It was only a matter of time until her electrifying writing style, powered by unapologetic intoxicating magic guaranteed to cast a spell on anyone, would reach the eyes of the public. Such ambition is what eventually landed her extraordinary success. All her books resonate with everyone, from the young to the old, with diverse cultures, languages, and religions worldwide. Above all, they act as a great source of information, tackling numerous taboo subjects people avoid.

Barbara Cartland's influence on her craft guarantees that she will inspire revolutionaries of the social world to develop powerful guiding principles. Her active engagement with the media and relentless self-promotion transformed her from a literary figure to a poignant cultural icon. Moreover, Cartland's adaptability aided in her perpetual relevance in the ever-changing world of literature. She travelled across different historical periods and social settings, ensuring her works would practically appeal to the changing modern audience. With her numerous philanthropic works and charitable activities, Cartland further cemented her legacy as a multifaceted social influencer who strategically utilised her influence for issues she strongly championed. Ultimately, it was clear that, whether they loved or hated them, Barbara Cartland wrote romance novels that shaped the industry and transformed the lives of countless women writers and readers.

# Cartland's Signature Style

As a writer, Barbara Cartland is known for her distinctive style. Her approach to romance literature remains imprinted in the collective memory, transforming the genre into a multimillion-pound industry. Part of her style features the portrayal of heroines from aristocratic families who lovingly and obstinately face the societal challenges of their times. Cartland's books are lavish, whether the stage or historical settings, breathtaking views in the surroundings, or overwhelming elements richly embroidered with elegant décor, and they lovingly immerse readers into the oases of beauty and romance. Her subtle and eloquent words join and express love and decorum, capturing the reader's fantasy.

Cartland's listeners and readers are also amazed by her skilful construction of plots with surprises full of twists, which have interesting themes that simultaneously provide emotional and intellectual challenges. Cartland has long been known as a great storyteller and evokes for readers the comfort of understanding the profound joy and pain of deeply human emotions. This sincere bond between people makes these books not just novels but stories that every person would love to read for the ride, multiplied by love, honour and defiance. In recent times, Cartland has been recognised as the leading author of romances free of explicit content and violence, which upheld idealistic morals.

Her love for depicting love as a powerful change agent while striving to preserve innocence became a hallmark of her writing, endearing her to those yearning for sweet and uplifting stories during shifting literary tastes. Ultimately, Cartland's lasting imprint on literature, infused with her unique blend of romance and morality, has established her legacy as a pioneer in creating timeless, refined, dream-like narratives that continue to captivate countless readers throughout the decades.

## A Legacy Beyond Literature

The impact of Barbara Cartland stretches well past the borders of literature, defining an enduring legacy that has literally touched multiple areas of culture and society. Cartland's name invokes images of smashing bestsellers in romance novels or reading entrancing narratives, but her influence goes beyond her writing into different spheres of dominion. One such area is fashion and style. The way she dressed—goodness did she dress herself; in her flamboyant pinks, there was an allure of fierce vanity and a unique take towards life. She softened the harsh strife of femininity and elegance by serving countless individuals willing to embrace an unapologetically confident posture toward an evolving society. Moreover, her timeless romance and traditional advocacy have sparked a renewed embrace of vintage fashion and etiquette, impacting modern aspects in one way or another.

What is more, Cartland's prowess as a social figure also helped cement her legacy, considering the outrageous extent of her influence multi-dimensionally. She was most known through her television and radio shows, and I must admit that engaging in public speaking served her purpose of imparting wisdom and inspiration worldwide. She single-handedly imprinted the image of a cultural icon.

In addition to her narrative creations, her charitable activities depict a kind and sympathetic side of her character, which was previously unknown. According to her friends, Cartland became philanthropically active and devoted much of her wealth to medical research, welfare programmes, and the arts. This underscores her status as an intricate and caring figure devoted to bettering humanity. Some aspects of Cartland's life dedicated to literature include her role as a guide and an idol, which form a substantial part of her legacy. She did not only portray fictional characters but also addressed real people and offered them genuine advice regarding love, relationships, and behaviour. She did this so charmingly that audiences were mesmerised and continue to be influenced even now. She has changed attitudes towards courtship and chivalry in a way that will sustain her for many generations. It is important not to forget her influence on popular culture and entertainment. Many of Cartland's novels have been adapted for film, demonstrating the enduring quality of these stories. Her command of language and commitment to writing captivating stories means that her superb work will have to be retold time after time through numerous mediums. To sum up, the life of Barbara Cartland is much more than the pages of her books, which makes her truly special.

Her multifaceted impact includes fashion, advocacy, mentorship, and entertainment, all of which resonate with people of varying ages and cultures around the world.

## Understanding Cartland's Work

Cartland's work is significant in the scope of literature and culture; her contributions have undeniably impacted modern romance. Any engagement with her life and works should begin with an overview as an entry point illustrating the variety of issues to be uncovered.

In its most basic form, an introductory paragraph aids in constructing the understanding of Cartland's influence on romance fiction. It captures her influence on love, courtship, and womanhood. Furthermore, exploring the themes and narratives of her works, the subject of admiration by countless generations should be prepared for in the introduction.

Navigating the critical discourse on Cartland's works encapsulated in the introduction highlights her treatment as a subject of praise, critique, or scholarly discourse. Assessing the intersection of literary merit and commercial success unveils Cartland's place within the greater literary world, emphasising the balance between empathetic adoration and nit-picky disdain over her artistic accomplishments.

By attending studiously to the conventions of popular literature, including bestsellers, romance may be placed on the lowest margin of artistry. The introduction should also highlight how her extensive career moulded the genre and created a stride for culture in the face of overwhelming social contempt, focusing specifically on her controversial positioning and redemption of the popular literature genre. Through this lens, all work put forth for adoration, critique, and dismembering solely for existing has earned its merit.

Ultimately, the introduction serves the important function of paying tribute to Barbara Cartland's lasting power by framing her as a literary figure whose impact goes far beyond the boundaries of the term. It paves the way for a detailed analysis of her multifaceted legacy. It invites the audience to recognise the intricacies of her storytelling and the enduring import of her romantic novels.

# Early Life and Influences

## FROM BIRMINGHAM TO SOCIETY'S SPOTLIGHT

### Birmingham's Blossoming: A Birthplace of Inspiration

Birmingham, the industrial city where Barbara Cartland was born, was not just a city of factories and machines, but a vibrant backdrop of her upbringing. Its rich history of industry and entrepreneurship, coupled with a modern centre of invention, made it a unique birthplace. The metropolitan energy and industrial innovation of Birmingham likely served as a unique source of inspiration for Cartland's literary works.

Barbara Cartland's formative years in Birmingham were a tapestry of unique experiences. The city, a hub of economic activity and working-class culture, offered her a vibrant and bustling environment. Her exposure to the city's opportunities and the resilience of its citizens left an indelible mark on her, instilling a strong sense of grit.

Birmingham's unique multicultural structure, a product of immigration and cultural influence, provided Cartland with diverse exposure to various cultures and traditions. This exposure to new ideas, beliefs, and customs fostered her character's compassionate depiction of the cultures that ensconced her romances.

The Victorian architecture of Birmingham, with its industrial twist, profoundly influenced Barbara Cartland's aesthetic senses. The embellished spires of St. Philip's Cathedral and the Jewellery Quarter captivated her, inspiring an appreciation for charm and sophistication that would echo in her literary works.

As noted earlier, Barbara Cartland's life in Birmingham was multifaceted, giving her unique experiences that shaped her understanding, provided a foundation for creativity, and nurtured the sensibility that marked her literary career. More than a mere industrial powerhouse, the steel-crafted city served as a wellspring of motivation, empowering and inspiring Cartland as she made her way from Birmingham to the limelight.

# The Cartland Family Lineage: Ancestral Influence and Heritage

Barbara Cartland had an illustrious family background, with many notable figures who left a significant impact on history. The Cartland family's ancestral influence and heritage played a major role in transforming Barbara into a literary figure. Their noble history, steeped in acts of gallantry, creativity, and scholarship, shaped her as a writer.

Among these figures is Major Bertram Cartland, Barbara's father, whose extraordinary military service made him a notable person in the Cartland family. His remarkable service made him a model of duty and honour for the family. His discipline and chivalrous nature certainly shaped Barbara's childhood upbringing, nurturing within her an appreciation for honour and bravery.

Moreover, Barbara's ancestors were respected as scholars, and, as such, their intellectual strength resonated throughout her family tree. This rich familial history and their appreciation for scholarly work paved the way for Barbara to embrace writing and storytelling, which was further proof of the impact her family had upon her life.

The Cartlands' philanthropic and public service commitment also shaped Barbara's sense of charity and duty. Generations of Cartlands lent their attention to charitable causes, providing Barbara with a firm grasp on focusing her compassion on creating a positive social impact.

Understanding the Cartland family tree allows for a comprehensive understanding of the people and events that impacted Barbara Cartland's life. The infusion of military service, scholarly pursuits, philanthropy, and the arts created layers of heritage that shaped her life and work and deeply impacted her ability to etch an indelible mark on the world of romance literature and societal philanthropy.

## Childhood Endeavours: Seeds of Storytelling

Barbara Cartland's passion for storytelling can be traced back to her childhood, when she demonstrated incredible curiosity and creativity, allowing her to devise captivating stories. This seeded her future potential as an indelible piece of literature. Cartland's passion for telling stories was enhanced by her reading habits and the people and events surrounding her. She seemed to be particularly sensitive to the emotions that were rife in her environment, which bloomed with vivid experiences during her early life. Furthermore, her childhood nurtured her unyielding spirit for overwhelming readers throughout the generations with wondrous powers of imagination. Through captivating worlds of adventure, romance, and enchantment, the alluring lives of ever-curious characters beckoned readers. The telling flows like spellbound dancing doors with thrilling exhilaration. Moreover, framed scenes of her foray adventures polished the hallmark ethos that her writings in her later years will uphold. These tools set and furnished her shape a legacy devoid of nightmares and suffused by sweet dreams. It would eventually be an emblem of her character. In unison, all these experiences and aspects manifested towards her writings, forming an exquisite legacy that still widely resonates today and won't vanish anytime soon.

Her storytelling efforts as a child are of great significance as they are a glimpse of the magic that would later characterise her works; her stories evoked emotions, kindled hopes, and provided comfort during the trials and tribulations of life. Simply put, Cartland's childhood exploits prepared both herself and the world for the vast myriad of adventures and romance that would fill her literary masterpieces.

# Education and Enlightenment: Foundations of Intellect

Barbara Cartland's early life was characterised by a devotion to schooling and an insatiable quest for knowledge which would aid her in the future. At a time when women were given constrained access to schooling, the pursuit of Cartland's intellectual growth was rather out of the box for her time. Her initial education provided the foundation for her commitment to learning, which later resulted in her becoming a renowned author and influential figure.

From a young age, Cartland mastered everything with consistent effort and a particular interest in academics. The syllabus alone gave her a basic grasp of various subjects such as literature, history, and languages, which helped her later in life with her numerous writings. Her exposure to classical literature and famous authors at that time greatly fanned the flames of her imagination and creativity, contributing to her potential endeavours of writing novel romances.

With the social constraints of Edwardian England, Cartland's zeal and focus on education demonstrated her independence and determination during that time. Her pursuit of knowledge alongside the rest of the world due to her education gave her a break from the shackles imposed on women. Thanks to mentors who guided her, she could immerse herself in intellectual pursuits, which was extremely liberating and enlightening.

Moreover, her education aided Cartland in acquiring knowledge regarding the different aspects and components of life, such as society and culture, at a global level. Her academic endeavours provided her with an understanding of the relative history, social situation, and world shift during her time, which greatly heightened her awareness and would later refine her writing skills, character construction, and plots in her novels.

Fundamentally, Cartland's intellectual underpinnings in her formative years not only sharpened her mind but also nurtured her ability to feel, appreciate, and possess an authentic grasp of humanity. This phase of her intellectual growth set the stage for her subsequent literary accomplishments that moulded her into a prophetic literateur with literary skill and insight into human life and existence.

## Societal Currents: Navigating Edwardian England

Social norms and values were undergoing a vigorous shift in the remarkable fabric of Edwardian England. The era stood as a crossroads of custom and advancement, witnessing substantial change within the boundaries of culture, politics, and society. As Barbara Cartland stepped into her childhood, she found herself trying to understand and cope with the changes in Edwardian society as they came.

One of the distinguishing features of Edwardian England's society was its class system, which was extremely rigid and affected every aspect of life. Cartland's life would encompass the glaring social inequalities between the aristocratic, new middle, and working classes. The stark differences in wealth, privilege, lifestyle, and access to opportunities would have profoundly shaped her perception of social order and the relationship between different social groups.

Likewise, the Edwardian Era saw the start of the suffragette movement as women fought for recognition and women's rights. Young Barbara, due to these factors, would have listened to passionate discussions about women's equality and the struggles and victories of the fight for women's suffrage and been inspired intellectually. Such influences would have motivated her to fight for women's issues and advocate for them through her writing and public appearances later in life.

In addition, lifestyles and perspectives changed drastically due to industrialisation and urbanisation. Alongside the increase in population, the promise of urban life and the ever-present charm of escaping to the countryside intensified. Cartland would have experienced both sides of the story—one that showcased progress and the other focused on preservation—during this time, and those lessons would help her understand the rapidly evolving society around her.

Furthermore, the Edwardian social context was characterised by growth in arts and literature. New innovative arts and intellectual activity were at their peak during this period, beginning with the captivating beauty of Art Nouveau and later including the Bloomsbury Group. For young Barbara Cartland, this would have certainly added to the many serendipitous decorators, sharpening her already growing intellectual curiosity due to the many philosophical debates.

Primarily, submerged and engulfed in the Cartland currents would serve as a melting pot of ideas that sculpted Barbara Cartland, thereby educating her with an appreciation of the complexities of society with progressive hope as well as heritage that would form her future writings during the Edwardian period.

## Fashioning the Future: Early Influences in Style and Grace

Her understanding of style and grace shaped Barbara Cartland's vision of the world from her formative years. The glamour of Edwardian England, where etiquette and order stood at the very centre of life, exposed young Barbara to the magnificence and sophistication bound to permeate her literary works. The surroundings that engulfed her were awash with sumptuous fabrics, impeccable manners, and lavish décor, all of which nurtured a deep-seated love for the arts - visual and fashion.

The Cartland era, a period marked by intricate dress patterns and upwardly mobile dancing flaunted by a specific social class, was a significant influence on Barbara's life. This era, which was a part of the Edwardian period, overshadowed her life. Everything from Edwardian fashion, with its intricate details meticulously crafted into sophisticated forms, to the social relations concerning manners, was a step toward understanding the complex world of appearances and reality. The upper class's wardrobe selections, dress etiquette, and the meanings inscribed within each article of clothing transcended mere decoration; they became important markers of identity and symbols of distinction.

To Cartland, the concept of grace went well beyond outward appearance. It also included a well-mannered refinement of one's speech, actions, and even interactions—an effortless grace fuelled by deep-rooted charm and goodness within. These early influences implanted in her the desire to aspire to live up to and encompass these ideals of grace, thus marking her in a way that would ultimately be realised through her literary heroines, who embodied such traits enchantingly.

When Cartland reached adulthood, the vestiges of her initial experiences with style and grace were fundamental building blocks for her personal and professional pursuits. The charm of high society's behaviour, clothing, and even their way of life was a constant source of creativity, granting her stories the much-needed finesse and magnetism. The intricate blend of prose and sophistication would mark her artistry, weaving strands of beauty, love, and idealised romance into timeless tapestries that captured readers' hearts for generations.

## Literary Inspirations: The Authors Who Shaped A Vision

Literary inspirations would stoke the fires of her vision during the early years of her life and nurture her love for storytelling, which, in turn, would undergo its evolution. Barbara, being a child, was willingly fostered and became associated with the works of authors, who, to put it simply, possessed an essence within their art that did not only touch the mind but delved deep into the soul, helping further in the development of her voice and writing. Among these authors, Jane Austen had a greater impact than the rest. She wielded an influence on Cartland's life as she filled her with the appreciation of the multifaceted human emotions alongside the intricate ballet of courtship and romance. The elegance, social critique, and the ever-so-important understanding of humanity would become a part of Cartland's literary universe, enabling her to give life to the mundane and let it flow into her books. As Cartland moved into the profound literary world of Britain, she was spellbound by the Baronet's wrought-worded historical novels, enabling the sprouting of her love for historical romance novels and teaching her the importance of vivid and elaborate settings anchored in reality. The Brontë sisters forged a new path and opened doors toward an elated side, and Cartland, alongside them, was inspired by their beautifully naïve tales of love, grief, and desire. As they told stories infused with deep feelings and raging passion, they profoundly impacted Cartland's development, guiding her towards the 'art' of storytelling and aspiring to mastery more akin to her age. Also, the enduring charm of Shakespeare's timeless tragedies and comedies absorbed by the back of Wharton's head enriched her stories with drama and beauty, like a bard, Cartland dramatised. The rest of Shakespeare was more elegant in certain multifaceted manifestations of the human soul.

Outside these figures, most notably, Elizabeth Gaskell, Thomas Hardy, and Henry James increasingly broadened her horizons and provided her with social character thematic friends. All these authors vehemently imparted to her the dream towards a unique space as a tonic novelist working within what was an unrocked inkwell.

# Family Dynamics: Parental Roles and Responsibilities

The structure of her family deeply influenced Barbara Cartland's evolving years. This discussion focuses on her parents' contributions to shaping her upbringing and literary career, which led her to success.

Sir Bertram Blofield Cartland, Barbara's father, was a renowned member of society and a military officer. His compassion mixed with sternness as a father softened Barbara's perspective towards discipline and honour. The broad exposure of Sir Bertram's worldly experiences and refined tastes educated his daughter on a number of cultural expressions, allowing her to develop into a connoisseur of style and sophistication. Lady Cartland, Barbara's mother, was the epitome of grace, poise and commendable charitable deeds. She nurtured Barbara's understanding of empathy and kindness, characteristics which resulted in her romantic tales. The

Cartland household entertained an environment where intellect, manifested in stimulating discussions and a love for learning, and etiquette, demonstrated in polite and respectful behavior, were highly regarded, which ultimately shaped Barbara's pursuits.

Her parents' expectations and aspirations greatly influenced the earlier ambitions and the sense of accomplishment that Barbara sought.

Barbara's ambitions in literature were fuelled by making a name for herself, a goal that was motivated by Sir Bertram's principles about preserving the family's reputation. His values instilled in her a sense of responsibility and a drive to excel. Encouragement from Lady Cartland helped foster Barbara's creative pursuits as she was gently steered by her ladyship, who unwaveringly supported her, into letting her imagination roam free in an environment where aspirations flourished and dreams blossomed. With her grasp of the intricacies of genteel society, Barbara was able to ascend through society's upper echelons as she learned the rules of upper-class behaviour and manners, showing that the aristocratic world was not alien to her.

Parental guidance interacted with personal traits and Barbara Cartland's character emerged, adding to her prose an exceptional mixture of old and new. Sir Bertram's discipline, instilled in her from a young age, shaped her into a determined and focused individual.

# Cultural Exposure: Theatre, Art, and the

## Allure of High Society

The rich and sophisticated society served as the background in which Barbara Cartland grew up, and it also provided her with productive formative years from an educational standpoint. She immersed herself in drama and wandered through art galleries, which helped her develop a sense of style and beauty that she later went on to exploit while writing her huge bestsellers based on romance and glamour.

All the theatre shows Cartland attended while growing up stimulated her imagination and gave her a newfound appreciation for performance art. Plays and operas taught her everything about dialogues, characters, and more, which would later become vital parts of her books. She learned to identify climactic moments during the story and capture the essence of drama and spectacle, which she later put into words in her novels.

Art influenced and enriched Cartland's worldview as she sought inspiration in the works of professional painters and sculptors and even in the passionate portrayals of people's portraits. The interplay of colour, shape, and even expression within art greatly inspired her as a writer. It enabled her to produce works filled with strong and clear images and descriptions, which were enhanced by the magnificence she found in different art pieces.

Additionally, the charm of the upper classes provided Cartland with a polished setting where refinement triumphed, civility flourished, and charm was exalted. In these high society circles, she learned etiquette, absorbed courtesy, noted social manners, and developed her love for the beauty of aristocracy, which infused her tapestry of literature with the sophistication and charm of high society.

All in all, the years of her childhood were probably the best years of her life because they offered her the most sophisticated artistic and cultural exposure, describing Cartland as a silky performance and the marvellous, dazzling strokes of art alongside the glamour of high society in a pantomime, would be more than merely accurate. These new forms were the foundation through which she poured her stories, ushering into them the beautiful fabrics of theatre, the elegant strokes of painting, and the otherworldly luxury that elevated her magnificent stories to the high peak of articulation.

## Ambitions Realised: Transitioning to London's Literary Scene

The move from Birmingham's pastoral charm to London's frenetic literary world marked an important turning point in young Barbara Cartland's life. For the first time, London's culturally and intellectually vibrant skyline allowed Cartland to immerse herself in the literary world and work towards her ambitions of becoming a published author. Bogged down by the literary giants that strode across the historic streets of London, young Cartland was spellbound. She navigated the city's literary circles and attempted to assert herself among the literary greats of the time. Her relentless willpower and stunning attributes helped Cartland overcome obstacles. Immersing herself in the art scene, the young woman was inspired by the exciting atmosphere of theatres, music halls, and art galleries. With zeal unmatched, London's literary circles single-handedly inspired Cartland's creativity and spurred her to rise to the challenge of achieving greatness in storytelling. Here, Cartland found the strength to nurture her creative gifts and became determined to succeed as a writer. Meeting the many challenges posed by publishers and literary professionals, she was finally able to pursue her goal of presenting her stories to others.

Nothing could deter her as she perfected her craft—and her stories resonated with the sentiments of time laced with ageless charm. The move to London instilled in Cartland an acute awareness of the power that words and stories could have, driving her towards painstaking literary mastery. As Cartland began to make her mark in the aristocratic literary society, her unique voice started to capture the praise and attention it so richly deserved through her captivating stories. The adventures beyond Birmingham were no longer mere journeys; they had transformed into a personal and literary quest to build a legacy that would delight readers for years to come. Long shifting her fantasies into reality, Cartland became the first woman to claim such a position in the heart of London, living as a timeless figure in the history of romance prose.

# A Tragic Beginning

## THE IMPACT OF WORLD WAR I

## A Historical Perspective: A World Ready to be Changed

In the early decades of the 1900s, the world was riddled with unrest. The European powers were associating and dissociating into pairs as the veins of Europe festered with nationalism. Everyone seemed to be on the verge of change as the wars and conflicts that came with industrial revolutions drastically shifted how millions had become accustomed to living prior.

Nonetheless, the rampant disparity and social inequities began splitting the delicate balance of society more and more, which ensured that spontaneous social revolutions were around the corner. Despite these issues being the underlying cause for change and progress, the grief-stricken world was embroiled in social conflicts that had become a perpetual timeless cycle of violence and grief.

This heated cauldron of abundant problems, waiting for an eruption that would redirect human history, was catalysed when Archduke Ferdinand was assassinated in 1914. As a result, conflicting nations around the globe declared war on one another, triggering a massive spiral of chaos that engulfed the continents.

What would be regarded as the Great War thrust the globe into an unprecedented whirlwind of chaos and destruction. How many lives were changed forever within the eye of the storm, with their aspirations quelled and reality shattering them like glass? The years leading to the rampant slaughter in World War 1 marked the absolute pinnacle of civilisation's greatest accomplishments, almost quaking with futile ambition. Even so, mankind was alive and waging a battle against their internal turmoil as they sought shelter from the storm. These were the warring times when Barbara Cartland, an English author, was motivated to start propelling her ideas onto paper and produce some of the finest written works in romance literature.

# The Great War: Overview of Turmoil and Transformation

Brought into existence in 1914 and lasting until 1918, the First World War marked a new chapter of violence and bloodshed for humanity. The Great War, which had been fought between European countries and their allies, marked a drastic dilution in power for these nations. Not only did the conflicts stay within Europe's borders, but the impact was notable worldwide. The war was not limited to the battlefield, as it took a toll on the economy, society, politics, and culture.

The devastation of trench warfare, military suffering, and human grief was reminiscent of the era's trench warfare. Mechanised weapons such as machine guns, tanks, and even poison gas were introduced significantly changing combat. The human toll alone was considerable, causing millions to be permanently scarred physically and mentally as survivors.

Domestically, the conflict had deep ramifications for people's daily lives. With the conscription of men into the military, women were forced to step into traditional work and home areas, marking a significant shift in societal norms. Control of destruction and order was difficult to manage as supplies were always low. The psychological blow of constant war, where every part of life is manipulated due to war, is very notable.

On an international scale and due to the war, empires fell, borders were redrawn, and new nation-states emerged. Additionally, Germany faced harsh consequences, contributing to future wars due to the Versailles Treaty of 1919. Not only did the conflict impact societies emotionally, but it altered their view on politics, identity, and existence.

In contrast, spaces for innovation and change emerged due to the tragedy of war. War reignited social changes, new technology, and medical advancements. Following the war, we witnessed the birth of several artistic and cultural movements and a global shift in power.

Despite the everlasting consequences of the Great War, it also taught us one thing: the resilience of mankind. Its impact will forever influence humanity and world events while darkening the 20th century.

# Family Affairs: The Cartland Household During Wartime

During the First World War, the Cartland family exemplified the societal changes and problems dealing with the war. The family underwent significant changes regarding dynamics as Major Bertram Falkner Cartland and Mary Hamilton kept wondering about the effects the war would have on their children. The father was also in the British Army fighting the war and was already facing the repercussions of service and combat. Major Cartland's wife grappled with a series of hurdles that accompanied her husband's absence due to the war. The sense of separation, as well as the deep-rooted anxiety of the family, was further aggravated by the strain of no clear resolution in sight. Apart from the domestic issues, death and even loss became constant companions. Apart from the use of grief, the Cartland children faced their own set of hurdles, and that was the absence of their father during prevailing depression combined with apprehension. This social setting provided the emotional climate for Barbara Cartland, shaping a young girl's understanding, values and ability to cope with difficulties.

The war thrust the Cartlands into new frontiers, disrupting their established roles and transforming their routines. The entire family unit felt the war experience, from rationing and resource allocation to the emotional and mental weight affecting each family member. Still, amid this turmoil, endurance and grit surfaced as the Cartlands came together to tackle the war's challenges. The dynamic interplay of personal strength and social responsibility alongside the enduring bonds of family emerged as core components forming the beliefs of Barbara Cartland, which later manifested in her writings. Grasping the complex dynamics within the Cartland family during the war offers a profound understanding of the aspects that moulded Barbara's character and led her to empathic and compassionate resilience. These qualities characterise her romantic tales.

# Loss and Resilience: Coping with Personal Tragedy

Barbara exhibited extraordinary strength growing up during the First World War. With loved ones lost as a result of the war, her scars would serve as emblems of her unwavering strength and grit.

Apart from sustained grief, forgettable agony also followed her family's path, giving them the unprecedented challenge of sailing through the unchartered waters of despair. The cushions of love and care, which were usually extended by her father and mother, became essential during these times. This resilience in the face of personal tragedy is a testament to the human spirit's ability to endure and overcome.

Everyone has encountered grief at some point; the same goes for the Addams. Epitomising the spirit of families from every corner of war-stricken Europe, they beautifully depicted struggles with grief wrapped in the blanket of ever-present adversity. With hands anchored beneath the warmth of suffering, their tale scribed on the pages of history speaks volumes about resilience.

Empathy and compassion, the seeds of empathy and compassion, were nurtured by personal tragedy, which deepened the understanding of the human experience that resonated within Barbara Cartland's literary works. During this phase of self-reflection and coping, she developed her character and developed the ability to formulate emotionally rich and real narratives. The impact of personal tragedy during the war years is equally underscored, as it has changed the perspective through which Cartland views the world and shaped her creative endeavours.

Appreciating the story of loss involving the Cartland family broadens the understanding of how personal tragedy affects the human spirit. It is a bleak reminder of the inner fortitude that can emerge from despair. Such motifs of conviction and hope that adversity can be withstood would later become cornerstones of Cartland's literary works as a reminder of the unrelenting legacy created by personal hardships and the will to recover.

## Broader Impacts: Societal Shifts and Gender Roles

World War I impacted society well beyond the battlefield. As men went overseas to fight, women began working in war-supporting positions, giving nurses and other industrial workers more responsibilities, which changed society. Women were also invited into factories to address the labour shortages caused by men enlisting in the military. This changed the economic landscape and began challenging previously held beliefs about women's societal role by advocating for their rights.

The aftereffects of the war continued to shape sociopolitical movements and cultural attitudes. The struggle for women's suffrage was deeply influenced by the fact that women could contribute significantly during wartime, proving their worth and ability for much more than house planning. Women surged into newsrooms, advocating for women's issues, extending the fight against social injustices and later turning into an international revolution. Subsequently, women like Barbara Cartland, who witnessed all this, began to focus on such issues impacts on women, influencing her writing and thus altering perceptions, portraying women as resilient and self-sufficient.

In addition, the war also created a new perspective towards the understanding of masculinity, especially in correlation to fighting and heroic feats of courage. The combination of psychological warfare and the loss of an entire generation of men led to contemplation regarding the structuring of masculine gender identities. Love and relationship studies that Cartland focuses on during periods of social change are centred on this greater context and feature male protagonists who not only embody the traits of the warrior paradigm but also of a soft-hearted civilisation. Through this, she encouraged conversations on sensitive and radical shifts in defined social standards of manhood, particularly concerning males in romance fiction.

Analysing the consequences of World War I on a larger scale brings to light issues related to the shift in social customs and gender roles and how they interconnect. It reveals how the drastic changes in one's world during this period set the stage for profound developmental adjustments in the 20th century. Cartland stood out as a strong advocate for upliftment during such transformative times through storytelling, progressive inclusivity, and empowerment.

## Experiencing the Front: Correspondence

## and Chronicles

Amidst the tumultuous backdrop of World War I, Barbara Cartland's experiences and observations were not confined to the domestic sphere. Engaging in extensive correspondence with individuals involved in the war effort, Cartland gained firsthand insights into the harsh realities faced by soldiers on the front lines. Through letters, she received vivid accounts of the battlefield, the camaraderie among troops, and the anguish of separation from loved ones. These deeply personal narratives were invaluable for her understanding of the human condition during wartime. Cartland also diligently chronicled her perspectives and impressions of the era in journals and diaries. These thoughtful reflections delved into conflict's emotional and psychological impact on individuals and communities. As her literary talents began to blossom, these recorded musings afforded her a wealth of poignant material to infuse into her future works of fiction.

Furthermore, documenting the war years served a dual purpose for Cartland—it provided an outlet for her emotional processing and created a substantial historical archive fueling her later literary endeavours. Her firsthand encounters with the stark realities of war instilled a profound sense of empathy and a commitment to preserving the untold stories of courage and resilience she encountered. The culmination of Cartland's immersive experiences and documentation from the war period is evident in the nuanced portrayal of the human spirit in her novels. Her keen observations and empathetic understanding of the psychological toll of war permeate her literary works, captivating readers with their authenticity and emotional depth. By integrating the voices of those who endured the war, Cartland imbued her romance narratives with a rich tapestry of genuine sentiment and historical realism, elevating her storytelling to a profound resonance. Ultimately, the connections fostered through correspondence and the chronicles borne of her reflections became instrumental in shaping Cartland's literary legacy. Armed with these intimate portrayals of the human experience during wartime, she could craft narratives that entertained and honoured the indomitable human spirit, forever cementing her status as a preeminent figure in romance literature.

# Philanthropy and Service: Contributions Beyond Writing

Barbara Cartland, fervently dedicated to aiding those affected by the turmoil of World War I, ventured beyond the realm of literature to enact tangible change in the lives of individuals and communities. In the wake of the war's devastation, Cartland engaged in various philanthropic initiatives to provide relief and support to those in need. Her compassionate endeavours extended beyond the literary sphere, underpinning her commitment to alleviating suffering and fostering hope amidst the post-war landscape. One of Cartland's prominent charitable pursuits was focused on assisting war veterans in their transition to civilian life. Recognising the profound challenges faced by returning soldiers, she took it upon herself to establish rehabilitation programs and vocational training opportunities.

Cartland sought to empower veterans with the necessary skills and resources to rebuild their lives and reintegrate into society with dignity and purpose by championing these initiatives. Moreover, inspired by her deep empathy towards war-affected families, Cartland initiated relief efforts aimed at providing essential provisions and support to widows and orphans left bereft by the conflict. Through fundraising campaigns and collaboration with charitable organisations, she endeavoured to ameliorate the plight of these vulnerable individuals, offering them solace and sustenance during their times of hardship.

Beyond addressing the immediate consequences of war, Cartland's philanthropic endeavours also encompassed endeavours that aimed at fostering a sense of healing and optimism within communities scarred by the conflict. She spearheaded cultural and artistic initiatives to revive the communal spirit and revitalise morale. Cartland played a pivotal role in nurturing war-affected populations' emotional and psychological recovery by championing the importance of creativity and beauty as essential components of human resilience. An integral part of Cartland's philanthropic legacy was her relentless advocacy for humanitarian causes and social equality.

Recognising the imperative of safeguarding the rights and well-being of all members of society, she actively voiced her support for initiatives promoting social justice and inclusivity. Her unwavering dedication to uplifting marginalised communities and advancing progressive societal changes further epitomised her embodiment of philanthropy beyond the constraints of conventional expectations. Ultimately, Barbara Cartland's commitment to philanthropy and service transcended the boundaries of her literary renown, exemplifying her enduring impact as a compassionate advocate for positive transformation. Her multifaceted contributions beyond writing echoed her altruistic spirit. They underscored her unwavering devotion to amplifying the voices of the marginalised and nurturing a world imbued with empathy, resilience, and unwavering hope.

## The Emotional Toll: Cartland's Reflections

Barbara Cartland's prolific literary career thrived amidst an era marred by the widespread aftermath of World War I. The lingering impact of this catastrophic event, which cost millions of lives and shattered countless families, left an indelible mark on Cartland's psyche.

Reflecting on her personal experiences, Cartland eloquently communicates the profound sorrow and anguish that enveloped her world during this unparalleled period of adversity. Her candid recollections offer a rare glimpse into the inner turmoil she grappled with in the wake of unimaginable loss and devastation. Furthermore, Cartland's introspective reflections shed light on her unwavering resilience, inspiring and instilling hope in readers.

While navigating the turbulent emotional landscape shaped by the war, Cartland adeptly weaves a narrative of unyielding fortitude and unfaltering determination, encapsulating the essence of her poignant storytelling.

Cartland synthesises the agony of war with the healing balm of romance through the prism of her anguish, infusing her narratives with an authentic depth born of profound emotional introspection.

# Literary Context: How Trauma Informs Romance

Trauma, whether personal or collective, profoundly impacts the human psyche. As a prolific romance author, Barbara Cartland masterfully intertwines trauma's complexities with the transformative power of love in her literary works. Through an exploration of her novels, it becomes evident that the author's experiences during World War I greatly influenced her portrayal of love and resilience within historical contexts. Cartland's ability to infuse her narratives with the emotional aftermath of trauma creates a compelling dynamic within her romance stories.

In examining Cartland's literary oeuvre, one can discern the delicate balance between portraying the effects of trauma and the pursuit of enduring love. The trauma experienced by characters often catalyses their journey towards emotional healing and ultimate fulfilment. This thematic underpinning reflects Cartland's astute understanding of human psychology and the complexities of overcoming adversity. Moreover, Cartland effectively captures the essence of resilience amidst tragedy and chaos through her vivid depiction of post-war societies and the lingering scars of conflict. Readers bear witness to the intricacies of trauma and its implications on romantic relationships within the nuances of Cartland's narratives.

The renditions of love in the face of adversity convey the indomitable spirit of the human heart and the transformative capacity of romantic connections. Cartland's adeptness at merging the harsh realities of trauma with the transcendent power of love establishes a deeply resonant thematic tapestry within her literature. As readers delve into Cartland's works, they are invited to traverse an emotional terrain that deftly illustrates how trauma informs one's perception of romance. Drawing from her encounters with loss and hardship, the author imbues her stories with a profound sense of authenticity and empathy. By delving into the psychological ramifications of trauma, Cartland constructs narratives that poignantly exemplify the resilience and emotional fortitude necessary for love to flourish amidst adversity. Ultimately, Cartland's exploration of how trauma informs romance is a testament to the enduring nature of love in the wake of despair. Her literature deftly portrays the intricate interplay between trauma and love, offering readers a poignant and enriching journey through the complexities of the human heart.

## Bridging to Creativity: From Loss to Literary Inspiration

Many authors undergo a profound journey from personal loss to literary inspiration. In Barbara Cartland's case, World War I's impact on her life and experiences catalysed her creative endeavours. The transformative power of loss can be observed in how Cartland channelled her emotions and experiences into her writing, reshaping her sorrow into captivating narratives of romance and hope.

Her passion for storytelling became a means of coping with her grief and connecting with others who sought solace and escape through her novels. By infusing her tales with an essence of resilience and optimism, she provided readers with narratives that resonated deeply in a post-war society, seeking comfort and reassurance. Cartland's ability to bridge tragedy to creativity was rooted in her keen observation of human emotion and unwavering belief in love's transformative power.

Through her writing, she skillfully wove themes of healing, redemption, and enduring love, drawing from the depths of her own experiences to create relatable and heartfelt stories that continue to captivate audiences across generations. Moreover, crafting these narratives gave Cartland an avenue for self-expression and empowerment at a time when societal norms often constrained women's voices and ambitions. Despite her challenges, her ability to carve a space for herself within the world of literature served as an inspiring example to many aspiring writers and individuals striving to overcome adversity. After exploring the delicate balance between personal grief and artistic innovation, we better know how individuals like Barbara Cartland transform their pain into timeless literary creations. By examining the emotional and psychological dynamics at play, we gain a deeper understanding of the profound impact of personal experiences on the literary landscape and the enduring legacy of resilience and creativity in the face of adversity.

# First Steps in Literature

## THE MAKING OF A ROMANCE ICON

## Navigating a Post-War World: The Literary Landscape

World War I left a mark on the world that was both intricate and dynamic, particularly for authors trying to make sense of the world. The shift brought about by the aftermath of the war impacted societal values, outlooks, and even literature in one way or another. Writers worked in a deeply introspective and disillusioned landscape characterised by a hope for renewal. This backdrop was immensely overwhelming, leading many writers and authors to attempt to understand and make sense of the changes in the world. Literature is not just a void space ready to be filled, but rather a picture of people's thoughts and feelings shaped by trauma and the transformation brought by the war. Authors during this time struggled with both expressing raw feelings and emotions devoid of sugarcoating while, at the same time, offering a glimmer of hope to their readers. The unprecedented longing for normalcy alongside uncertainty forced writers and authors to tell stories that mirror people's feelings and conditions, catering comfort and understanding to a society longing for hope after the debilitating conflict.

Therefore, the literature milieu after the wars served as a melting pot for creativity, testing one's limits and the search for the true essence of a story. A rich tapestry of differing perspectives and voices emerged with the profound changes during this time, catering to the ever-renewing hunger for literature that delves deep into one's actions and captivates the audience during the war while providing hope for a better tomorrow. Those authors during the fresher periods after the war fiercely sought new themes within their literature, allowing for a vivid surge in self-expression among new uprising authors. Unfortunately, this does not serve as the final revelation, as all of this served the purpose of helping these upcoming novelists turn into pioneers during a time filled with chaos, reliance and an unending need to find the purpose behind it all.

# The Power of Prolificacy: Early Writings and Themes

Barbara Cartland's initial steps in prose carving would make her a financial titan of romance fiction. Her sheer devotion to telling her stories contributed to the exquisite number of novels this prolific author managed to produce during this period. Understanding the various themes that shaped her literary imagination gives us a glimpse into the background of her literary life. The contours of her view of humanity as a thinking animal were deep and profound, and she marvellously spun tales about its inspirations and consequences.

Some of the most spectacular strands of her imagination strived to take shape around love's triumph against insurmountable odds, lust demarcating country lines and the lovers being citizens of opposing nations. Capitalising on these tenets, Cartland ensured she could sprinkle earnest and unpretentious feelings amid her work to guarantee its acceptance, thus ushering the fiction world into a new era. Adding to this was her respect and admiration for strong women portrayed as brave and virtuous leading ladies alongside equally virtuous gentlemen commanders, establishing an encouraging path of civilised masculinity in fiction.

Cartland's early writings were also marked by her sharp attention to the social sphere. She studiously commented on the gaps in society's hierarchy in terms of divisions of class, the role of femininity, and the ability of love to shatter social barriers.

Her readers did not seek romantic escapism but thoughtful reflections on human life; thus, her nuanced approach captured their attention. She used eloquent prose, vivid characterisations, and her masterful understanding of the complexities of human nature and nuances so that her stories would resonate with a large audience.

During tumultuous times, Cartland's stories served as a beacon of hope and a source of optimism for her readers. Her belief in the invincibility of love and the human heart was evident in her work, inspiring countless readers through empathy, compassion, and resilience. Her compelling novels were a testament to the enduring power of love, offering her readers a sense of hope and a reminder of the indomitable human spirit.

Barbara Cartland's prolificacy is manifested in two ways in her works: the sheer volume of her output and the enduring themes and narratives of her work. Her ability to captivate the imaginations of countless readers and lay the foundation of the romance genre for future generations of writers is a testament to the lasting impact of her work. Her influence continues to be felt in the world of literature, shaping the way we understand and appreciate romance novels.

## Defining the Genre: Conventions of Early Romance Novels

Understanding the history of romance literature requires one to pay attention to the basic conventions that form early romance novels. These conventions give the foundation for the genre, even if they undergo some changes with time. Conventions pertaining to romantic love as a powerful and passion-filled entity that transforms people typically take precedence because of societal problems and expectations. These societal problems and expectations, such as the role of women in society and the constraints of class divisions, heavily influenced the early romance novels. Chivalry, courtly love, the seeking of perfection in people and places, and escapism are common traits associated with early romance novels. Further, the combination of women as virtuous and morally strong characters, who experience emotionally deep and complex journeys while being entangled in multifaceted narratives, gives romance literature its timeless appeal.

Class barriers, misunderstandings, or opposition from family members enrich the emotional conflict of the narratives. The deep emotional connection associated with the characters' struggles to escape the stifling barriers placed upon them is unforgettable. Also, by portraying delightful places where love inevitably triumphs over obstacles, these books have become a fundamental part of the genre. Additionally, gardens and estates are just a couple of examples of the romantic symbols and imagery embedded within the plot.

These factors all contribute to the framework of early romance novels, which simultaneously attempt to garner a reader's attention, set expectations, and pave a path for subsequent novels.

## Publishing Milestones: Breakthrough Works and Bestsellers

Barbara Cartland's career as a writer of romantic fiction included a plethora of milestones that aided in the establishment of her legacy within the literary world. During the initial phases of her career, Cartland underwent remarkable milestones in her creative and commercial endeavours, greatly achieving the world of romantic literature with her contributions.

One of Cartland's most notable accomplishments is 'Jigsaw,' published in the year 1934. This novel marked a change in Cartland's life as it not only reached significant sales but also received positive reviews from critics and fellow authors. 'Jigsaw' was not just a personal triumph for Cartland, but it also had a significant impact on the romance genre. Its enchantingly told tale and captivating characters set a new standard for romance fiction, showcasing Cartland's talent and propelling her amongst the vital literary elites. The success of 'Jigsaw' paved the way for a new era in romance literature, inspiring countless authors and captivating readers with its earnest and unpretentious feelings.

After the success of Jigsaw, Cartland went on to create a number of other bestsellers, including A Hazard of Hearts, Love in the Clouds, and The Wicked Marquis, solidifying her reputation as a widely known author. Unlike most authors, her works were listened to and accepted by audiences, and she quickly gained a loyal base.

Additionally, her unparalleled mastery in combining narratives with elements of romance garnered all the attention to her as a publishing powerhouse. Her novels received notoriety since they didn't follow rigid boundaries and were filled with original takes on romance, loyalty, and fate, which emotionally touched and greatly motivated readers for many years. She was also famed for her incredibly vivid imagery and imaginative and unforgettable heroines, which captured the hearts of millions and landed her numerous bestselling titles.

With growing success, Cartland delved into writing serialised stories and working with renowned magazines and periodicals, widening her audience base and solidifying her status as an esteemed bestselling author. 'The Secret Bridge' and 'A Royal Love Story' were some of the most popular magazine serialisations, boosting her public image and serving as a testament to her talent as a captivating storyteller. Readers were left enchanted after each instalment, paving the way for the massive success of her full-length novels.

Fundamentally, Barbara Cartland's publishing achievements epitomise her creativity, dedication to her profession, and impact on the world of romantic literature. Each of her breakthrough works and bestsellers offered testimony of her unmatched skill in capturing the hearts and minds of readers from every corner of the globe with tales of love and passion.

## Developing a Unique Voice: Stylistic Choices

Barbara Cartland's rise to a beleaguered icon of romance is inseparable from the evolution of her special voice and distinctive stylistic choices. As an author, she attempted to break away from the barriers of romantic fiction by designing her themes and plots with a touch of sophistication, optimism, and nostalgia.

Cartland's stylistic approach is best known for her depiction of love and romance in its truest forms. Unlike many of her peers, rather than relying on cynicism, she embraced an idealistic worldview of relationships. She sought to whisk her readers into a world of wonder and fantasy. This choice of celebrating love and the ideals associated with it managed to create a special bond with the audience that stood the test of time throughout her career.

Cartland was further adored for her skilful manipulation of language and imagery, through which she created rhythmic prose to dramatise the splendour of historical periods and lively romantic adventures. She vividly captured the details of history and furnished readers with rich images of elegant ballrooms, lavish estates, and turbulent landscapes where love had triumphed and troubled timelessly in all its glory and agony.

As much as Cartland was an outstanding storyteller, the description of her main protagonists and their traits showed that she uniquely stylised them by making them elegantly poised, virtuous, and loyal to duty. Her heroines were always courageous and strong, believing in love's ability to make an enduring change, while her heroes were protective, fiercely loving, and devoted to their lady. By placing characters with unchanging values, Cartland enchanted her audience and blessed them with timeless role models to look up to and strive to be.

Cartland's stylistic policies included, and were not limited to, her public persona and self-portrait as an author. Her love of high fashion, theatricality, and unapologetic self-promotion of romance as a sophisticated art made her fully embody her novels. This blend of life and art put together a biography of Cartland, which turned her into a British author and the personification of the ideal romantic advocate of her books.

She brought life to the characters she created. Because of that, her unparalleled self-expression transformed the foundations of romantic literature, profoundly advancing its scope in a way that allows timeless inspiration and delight for countless readers.

# The Role of Research: Historical Accuracy

## in Narrative

Historical accuracy in narratives is yet another facet of Barbara Cartland's literary mastery. Her romance novels, which spanned various historical periods and events, were sophisticated enough to reflect history, even as they stemmed from authentic research that transported readers centuries prior. Each detail, from clothing to manners of the people, was crafted carefully, ensuring an immersive experience into past eras.

Cartland did not merely scratch the surface regarding aesthetics; she tried her best to obtain the spirit of the different epochs as diverse after extensive research. Whether it was the majestic grandeur of Tudor courts or the explosion of Europe during the wars, the narratives always had an overwhelming authenticity. This enhanced the enjoyment of reading and offered praise from historians and fundamental critics for the contexts provided.

Finding and integrating accurate historical facts and information required extensive cross-discipline verification with specialists, which, in turn, posed challenges. Cartland was meticulous in her research and claimed that she mastered every detail of her plots, including the architecture, geography, and even the minutiae of everyday life. Such understanding enabled her to write with extraordinary imagination, allowing the readers to see and understand the complexities of ancient civilisations.

This care Cartland put into the historical reality of her books went as far as the conversation and words used in the pages, inscribing the language plot of her tales. She applied old phrases and sayings of certain times into the dialogues and interactions of the characters, which provided a greater level of realism to the social and character relations. Such devices not only take the readers to another time but also show the author's effort and care in trying to depict the real world of history.

Well-defined research and fact-checking strategies in historical reality make Barbara Cartland a pioneer in historical romance novels. Her attempts at remaining real while writing romances exceeding the boundaries set by the genre resulted in stories that will, for ages, prove the strength of written history. By working tirelessly to piece the real world together through research, Cartland marked her name with authority as the first to write such profoundly insightful historical fiction.

## Critical Reception: Praise, Criticism, and Interpretation

Barbara Cartland is a renowned novelist whose works have drawn the attention of critics in both a positive and negative light. Her garnered dual perception under the romance banner is impressive, and this must speak volumes about her writing capabilities.

Cartland's works showcase her strongest features, revealing her capacity to imagine settings such as love, honour, and extravagant locations and elegantly weave them into the narrative. Readers appreciate her fiction novels, regardless of the time frame, because of the global affection this form of literature receives. Her novels serve to strengthen and validate the assertion that there are hundreds of love-struck readers who admire anything and everything that Cartland writes. This widespread admiration is a testament to her significant contribution to the romance genre.

On the other hand, some scholars and critics have raised concerns about the formulaic plot lines and shallow character profiles that inhabit her stories. They argue that her novels often follow a predictable pattern, with characters that lack depth and complexity. Some vehemently oppose the romantic roles she clings to, arguing that they are outdated and not reflective of the intricate realities of modern-day relationships. Furthermore, she is also critiqued for the shallow portrayal of her characters and the utter predictability of her plots, alluding to the possibility that her extensive oeuvre is at the expense of substantive storytelling.

The nuances of interpreting Cartland's works are as diverse as the readers themselves. Many contemporaries regard her works wistfully, soothing themselves with sentiment and fantasies of yesteryears, while others deeply analyse the socio-cultural contexts encapsulated in her plots. Such sensibilities bestow upon her works the distinction of being timeless love stories, yet, with lesser grace, treat her with disdain as expository romantic notions put forth underlying social and gender ideology abdications in her works. This timeless quality of her works evokes a sense of nostalgia and appreciation for her storytelling.

The debate over Cartland's literary heritage unmistakably depicts her influence over the romance genre and literature history. Her work has shaped the romance genre and influenced the broader literary landscape. It is a testament to her ability to provoke multifaceted discussions—readers, intellectuals, and devotees are invited to consider the role of romantic literature in the backdrop of historical developments and the impact of her work's narrative arc and scope. In any case, the paradoxical yet unending discourse concerning the value of romance fiction and the reverberations it sends throughout literature is augmented by the equally diverse evaluations concerning Barbara Cartland's literary production.

## Overcoming Challenges: Persistence in Publishing

Publishing proved to be a challenging arena for Barbara Cartland, especially considering her talent as a writer. Barriers of all sorts came her way, which required immense effort to breach. A major roadblock for her was the stereotype surrounding romance literature that was prevalent during the early stages of her career.

During this time, the literary world was largely dominated by male authors, and themes of masculinity reigned supreme. Cartland's devotion to writing romances was met with scepticism and dismissal. Securing a publishing opportunity was severely hindered by the attitude that romance novels belonged to the realm of frivolity and were devoid of literary merit. However, unwavering in her dedication to her craft, Cartland stood her ground. Like many other writers, Cartland took on the burden of paying the romance genre's industry-wide baggage. She firmly argued that love stories served as much-needed doses of escapism to readers, which helped her overcome his adversities throughout her career. Having to navigate the intricacies of publishing, she had to deal with underestimation and rejection, including some publishers questioning her genre's marketability. Fortunately, her faith in romance fiction was enough to sustain her through such tumultuous times. Throughout, she experienced relentless rejection, and it took an abundance of tries before she could sharpen her craft and storytelling.

This relentless devotion to her craft set Cartland apart as a tenacious force enduring hardship. Further, Cartland's ability to shift with the market's evolving demands and reader interest helped sustain her publishing career. She continued to pay attention to the tides in the literary sea, adapting to changes while remembering the essence of romance that underpinned her writing. Through skilful manoeuvres and keen business strategies, she established lasting partnerships with publishers who understood the worth of her works. In the face of widespread derision directed toward romance fiction, most of Cartland's perseverance eventually paid off when she secured a lasting place in the world of literature. Her advocacy for the romance genre was not limited to her interests, as she fought for the value and merit of romance literature on an even wider level.

## Influences and Inspirations: From Classic to Contemporary

Barbara Cartland's rich, captivating novels on romance were professionally shaped by a game of division spanning from classic literature to contemporary societal trends. Throughout her lifetime, she seemed awe-inspired by great literary figures such as Jane Austen and Charlotte Brontë, as well as the Brontë sisters, incorporating their sophisticated prose and multifaceted character development into her works. These timeless texts served as the springboard for unending readers' generosity towards the enduring charm and romance the texts provided. Moreover, her all-encompassing inspiration from evolving social shifts and cultural movements during her lifetime offered fertile ground to draw inspiration. From the grandeur of the Roaring Twenties to the spirit displayed during World War II, Cartland seamlessly integrated societal dynamics into her works alongside the essence of each era. Drawing from such contemporary themes ensured her impeccable stories did not lose appeal and affection.

Cartland's real-life experiences and encounters fundamentally influenced her creativity. Their interactions and her travels to different parts of the world added new layers of culture and perspective to her storytelling. Such perspective was important because it allowed Cartland to add to her narratives many places, people, and traditions, thus making her books rich and captivating.

Furthermore, Cartland, a keen observer of life, also used psychology and sociology to understand relationships and feelings and bring emotions and dynamics to the page. Character Straight to the Pageers in her books has profound psychological depth and emotional resonance, undoubtedly resulting from deep knowledge about people's relationships and social systems. By combining fundamental elements of literature with modern-day society, Cartland achieved her status as a central icon in romance literature, which earned the love and admiration of millions of readers worldwide.

## Establishing an Identity: Branding Barbara Cartland

Barbara Cartland's greatness as a literary figure lies not only in her ability to write extensively but also in her ability to craft a brand around her name. For this purpose, she developed an image that defined her as a romantic, elegant, and glamorous woman. Cartland was the first to do such a thing, but she went above and beyond by creating an image of herself that turned her into a global literary star.

Cartland's brand and identity stemmed from her unique personal style. She dressed in a trademark pink gown, jewels, and immaculate hair. These factors became mainstays of her identity and firmly established in the minds of the public the attraction of romance associated with spearheading Barbara Cartland. She also made public appearances with her Pekingese dogs and her roses, reinforcing her identity as a romantic icon and captivating the hearts of many readers and audiences.

The brand was cultivated and gardened through modern media such as radio and television, print, and even post-branding reminders of her works. Later, her interviews and eloquent speeches attracted listeners and begged the question of how she isn't at the centre of love matters.

She effectively blended her life, insights, and personal experiences into her fiction, casting a spell that drew readers into her world with the captivating characters she created.

Aside from her physical appearance, Cartland's brand was well-known in other sectors, such as philanthropy and advocacy. Her engagement in various charitable causes, especially those aimed at children and animals, built depth to her public persona, making her appealing to people worldwide and earning her the title of a compassionate humanitarian.

Moreover, Cartland's astute marketing techniques were specially designed to appeal to people of all ages and cultures. Her enthralling historical novels are dominant, but the enduring themes of love, honour, and integrity encapsulated within them extend beyond borders, making her beloved worldwide. Cartland became an emblem of romance with these endeavours, deftly evolving beyond her novels into a cultural symbol that still inspires and captivates readers today.

Ultimately, Barbara Cartland's branding broadened her literary achievements and romantically enhanced her image simultaneously, which created an enduring mark on her literary works and popular culture.

By assuming the graceful elegance of romance and continuously reinventing herself, she crafted an impact that transcended the bounds of authorship and etched itself deep into the psyches of avid romantics.

# The Hallmark of Romance

## CRAFTING THE PERFECT HISTORICAL LOVE STORY

## Defining the Genre: Elements of a Timeless Romance

Romance novels are treasured for their ability to describe captivating stories with interesting backdrops and themes that endure everything. To define the genre means considering the timeless appeals and the universality of its core elements. Every memorable romance novel seems to have a carefully constructed blend of appealing tropes and themes that cater to different audiences. Enthralling tropes such as enemies to lovers, second chances, and forbidden love offer another window into captivating storytelling.

These archetypes currently in use take characters on emotional journeys through timeless conflicts, evoking feelings such as empathy from readers. Enduring themes, including the power of love, the quest for self-fulfilment, and the victory of hope against all odds, highlight humanity's underlying need for relationships, understanding, and fulfilment. From infatuations to lifelong commitments, the depiction of relationships allows readers to grasp the intricacies of emotions, fostering an unprecedented level of intimacy and connection. These universal ideas tell a captivating tale and shape them into profound commentaries on humanity. As devices that show man's condition, these elements are fundamental in crafting stories beyond entertainment.

They provide an escape and the achievement of goals, shaping a reality beyond imagination. They effortlessly lift readers from the mundane to vivid realms. A hallmark of enduring romantic novels is the timeless emotion they evoke alongside their ability to transport readers to different places and eras. With well-crafted tropes and themes, authors can create impactful stories that endure over time, cementing the importance of romance in literature.

## The Art of Historical Accuracy: Weaving Fact with Fiction

As I discussed before, one of the main inclusions of a historical romance novel lies in the author's skilful blend of factual writing and the world of fiction. Accomplishing this blend requires intense scrutiny, a little creativity, and a strong respect for the period in question. History serves as a skeleton for the body of the story: the work of fiction being given life has to be plausible and well-researched. There is much responsibility placed on the author, who has to lift readers to the scenes of the past and let them traverse history step by step, gap-free and unbiased.

Hence, achieving ethnographic accuracy requires comprehensively capturing the society's language, clothing, and spirit of the evaluated period. It requires analysing various pieces of history from documents, oral interviews, and publications to construct an accurate and captivating story. A harmonious fusion of fact and fiction requires events, notable people, and defining moments of history to be skillfully blended with creative expression permitted by the genre. Such a blend anchors the narrative and enhances the experience offered to the readers regarding the history being explored.

Moreover, historical accuracy allows modern audiences to understand and appreciate the countless subtleties and difficulties of life in the past, evoking empathy and compassion. Equally important, maintaining historical authenticity allows the reader to connect deeply with the story, shedding light on the core purpose of the narrative—to remain true to history. Balancing fact and fiction requires skill, but a form of dedication and respect characterises the genre of historical romance. This effort rewards the readers with something priceless and appealing—the strongest elements of history. Furthermore, maintaining accuracy brings powerful illusions that ease immersion into the story and build empathy to connect with the characters created.

# Character Development: Crafting Complex Protagonists

Protagonists in historical love novels need special attention towards character development to be intriguing. The protagonists serve as anchors around which readers revolve while experiencing how love defies time. To achieve this, authors must go beyond superficial characters to provide depth, authenticity and relatability. The character of complex protagonists refers to those individuals whose personalities and motivations change over time within the encompassing story arc.

They are not only archetypes concerning the concepts of heroism and the damsel in distress but also possess inner struggles along with hopes and weaknesses. Developing such characters requires researching their surroundings and the dynamics of their society during the relevant period and giving them traits that make them human concerning all timelines. One of the most important ways to develop a character is through internal conflicts, moral dilemmas, and actions in contrast to ethics. Authors can create strong emotional bonds between the protagonist and the readers by portraying a relatable struggle with ethical dilemmas. To achieve this outcome, one must look deep into the character's wants and fears and society's scope.

Moreover, developing complex protagonists means that every

character needs to straddle the fine line between two-dimensional and three-dimensional. They must be presented as products of several cultures, social norms, and historical events, cumulatively shaping who they become in the story. The criteria regarding the actions and decisions made are based on the character leading as a persona who understands the period profoundly, resonates and is well accepted by people of today's world. Furthermore, along with achieving complex protagonists comes the responsibility of defining relationships to formulate details around social connections. Relationships that are romantic, parental, and friendly towards heroes and heroines should be true to life in nature, thus refining the story's emotional impact. Respecting human complexity gives authors a reason to appeal to the readers' emotions and develop a connection with the protagonists. Lastly, combining history with humanity within a narrative will create sophistication within profound resonating characters attuned to different eras. Building emotional reflection allows romance to be an everlasting theme regardless of timelines. In reinforcing the foundation of historical romances, authors provide a canvas rich in stimuli with timeless stories to cherish throughout the ages. This further puts the remarkable fusion of history and human experiences, which tells the story of love.

## Romantic Tension: Building Suspense and Anticipation

Creating romantic tension captures the readers' attention and makes them feel strongly about the events of the story.

At its essence, this technique has effectively created anticipation, desire, and uncertainty, which drive the romantic tale forward. Audiences experience the struggles and the deep yearning between the characters and the plethora of misunderstandings. Through this lens, authors can portray the authentic intensity of their bond. In this genre, as romance unfolds within the confines of society and culture, it often becomes more complex and beautifully poignant as there are implied musings of what society considers appropriate. Romantic tension should be built on outlining emotions and intentions; in other words, romantic feelings must circulate around the characters for various reasons to make sense. Through compelling narration, the realisation of attraction and the tension which accompanies it can make readers spellbound. Such gentle and gradual revealing enables readers to feel emotions with the characters and provides a strong investment in the story.

Moreover, providing impactful internal thoughts and incorporating subtle body language heightened intimacy, creating deeper anticipation for the eventual meeting between the love-struck romantics. Hope and despair, a romance's most fundamental dichotomy, contribute to the fabric of romantic tension. Captivated by the emotional exuberance of the protagonists enduring chaotic events and overcoming impossible challenges, readers are put on a roller coaster ride full of highs and lows. Whether it is an attraction that is off-limits, an impending betrayal, or societal disapproval, these factors intensify the expectancy for characters to join forces and overcome conflicts. Fulfilling this oscillation of unfulfillable needs alongside potential heartbreak creates the ultimate suspense, captivating audiences' fantasies and connecting them deeply with heroes.

Furthermore, pacing and the placement of drama aid in mounting romantic tension. The smooth transition from vulnerability to raw emotion and back allows authors to make readers anticipate every single turn of the page. Using cliffhangers, almost-encounters, and steamy encounters cleverly guarantees heightened anticipation, mimicking the rhythm of the developing relationship.

This shifting rhythm builds into a breathtaking climax, astounding readers with relentless excitement and leaving them deeply committed to the resolution of the protagonists' romance.

In summary, constructing romantic tension in a historical love story is captivating because of the intricate process involved. The story's blend of emotions, challenges, and pacing allows writers to create exquisite tapestries that capture readers' passion. By fostering desire and anticipation, readers will feel and experience every rhythm of their hearts along with the readers who are captivated by their love.

# Emotional Depth: Eliciting Readers' Responses

This is how writers create captivating experiences. The emotional depth of a historical love story strengthens the author's attempt at capturing the reader's heart and gives them an unforgettable experience during and after immersion into the story. Authors utilise powerful emotions to try to reach a deep connection with the readers. One way to achieve deeper emotions is by evoking powerful sentiments and portraying real experiences that people can relate to. Characters going through relatable and challenging experiences add depth to the story. These experiences can include unreciprocated affection, hardships, relationship struggles, etc.

Exploring the protagonists' internal conflicts and their emotional fragility adds layers to the story. Authors diving deep into the inner turmoil of the characters' struggles, insecurities, fears, and hopes provide a more three-dimensional representation that can provoke empathy and self-reflection. Witnessing emotional journeys through the lens of various characters' emotions increases the likelihood of readers connecting to and becoming invested in the story.

Moreover, incorporating powerful sensory details into historical love stories also augments their emotional depth. By portraying vivid historical contexts, capturing their sights, sounds, and textures, and portraying them in such a manner, authors transport the readers into the story and let them navigate through the world's emotions in coherence with the characters. This sensory perspective not only enhances the impact of the emotion within the story but also brings the reader to a completely different time and space. Another way to stir readers' emotions is through the use of symbolism and metaphor, with careful consideration, to strategise them. Symbols and metaphors which are perceptively chosen have the power to convey far deeper emotions than intended, distinctively resonating within readers while presenting the narrative in a way that captivates unexplained imagination. These symbols connect readers emotionally to the story, transforming one's reflection into a great level of contemplation.

To conclude, crafting emotional complexity in love stories set in history demands a careful combination of human aspects, inner character clashes, immersive world-building, and deeper meaning. If executed successfully, this emotional complexity creates a bond between the audience and the story, which determines how impactful the story is. It makes the story stay within the heart and mind of the audience even after they finish the story.

# Dialogue Mastery: Authenticity and Period Language

Mastering period-specific dialogue is a crucial element in crafting a historical romance novel. It requires a deep understanding of cultural context and a keen appreciation for language. This mastery is essential for capturing the essence of bygone eras and immersing readers in an authentic narrative.

Authenticity in dialogue necessitates attention to contemporaneous formalities or slang, idioms used, and even etiquette. Shifts in address and manners of speaking must be blended together alongside vocabulary to create an experience that feels as if one is living in the world while also being understandable. Achieving accuracy while balancing relatability requires exceptional dialogue mastery.

In addition to culture, societal branches also add authenticity to period dialogue. Disparate social classes, changing customs over time, regional accents, and their evolution contribute to the historical language mosaic. The characters' identities, dreams, limitations, and struggles form the backdrop of their interactions. The dialogue reveals the motivations behind their relationships and conflicts. Incorporating dialect and regional word choices enriches the plot while bringing life to characters and capturing the time's atmosphere. It is also essential to avoid any bias towards modern perception and build a blend that resonates with today's audience while maintaining historical accuracy. Achievable engagement is possible with a thoughtful mixture of period language and contemporary recognition.

Furthermore, dialogue is a powerful tool of thematic expression and emotional insight. It conveys the spirit of the time and the characters' struggles and feelings towards one another. Through the give-and-take of discussions, the audience views the interwoven realities of love and honour and the social constructs, which form the plot's essence and propel its emotional depth.

As with any skill, mastery of period-specific dialogue requires knowledge of historical language complemented by a sharp literary eye to balance accuracy against modern ease. The author's effort to render a character's past through captivating language crafted for readers passionate about historical romances reveals a delightful read.

## Setting the Scene: Creating a Vivid Historical Backdrop

In historical romance novels, the setting is not just a backdrop but a character in its own right. The author's skill in portraying the setting truly immerses readers into a different period and era. Whether it's the ballrooms of Regency England or the rugged Scottish Highlands, each setting is rich in historical narratives.

To achieve this, the writer should explore history with excitement and curiosity, developing relevance to the details they plan to use in the narrative. This includes researching the era's architecture, fashion, social customs, and dominant viewpoints. Accurate details enhance the quality and authenticity of the story. At the same time, prose allows the reader's imagination to take over and rejoice in the beauty of a palace or an Industrial Revolution-era city full of life and movement.

Sensory language constructs a multi-layered picture in which sight, touch, smell, and hearing can all be appreciated. It transforms the setting into one that can be felt by adding texture, smell, and background sounds, enhancing the reading experience and immersing the reader in the historical world.

Moreover, historical scenery offers a platform for the characters' performances, influencing the plot and character development. The setting can highlight societal norms, political turmoil, or cultural milestones, deepening the storyline. A well-crafted historical setting heightens the emotional conflict for the main characters and increases the reader's investment.

In summary, insightful descriptions of historical settings in romance novels go beyond just a description and contribute toward setting motivation character dynamics and enabling the reader to resonate with the text. This invites writers to actively seek true historical references because doing so transports readers into the beauty and spectacle of history, fostering a sense of connection and investment in the narrative.

# Plot Structure: Balancing Pace and Depth

Creating a plot structure for a historical love tale that truly captivates readers requires a delicate balance. It is crucial to maintain emotional depth while ensuring the pace is fluid and engaging. This balance ensures that the audience fully engages with the story, digesting the interrelationships among characters and the historical setting through the well-defined plot framework.

Pacing in a plot structure requires managing all areas of a particular story. Quieter intervals should be sandwiched between intense moments full of actions, high stakes, and bursting with emotions, and the opposite also rings true. These waves of rhythm, dynamic, engrossing stimuli, and emotional relativism allow the audience to funnel full attention towards the characters while simultaneously building expectations for amazing outcomes and cliff-hanging resolutions. From a gripping secret revelation to an awe-inspiring forbidden love story, keeping the audience engaged while building tension is the crux of pacing.

The level of intricacy of the plot is also important. Readers are more inclined to appreciate a storyline incorporating historical context, a character's deep reasoning for actions, and a thematic framework. A simple romantic story can be turned into a complex and thought-provoking narrative about human nature and emotions through subplots, intricacies, and authenticity while maintaining a rich historical context.

When attempting to achieve balance in a plot's structure, intertwining romance, history, and character development into a singular narrative collage of flowing moments is key. All elements should bolster the central story without straying from the historical setting. Romance and history must be symbiotically woven into the story's framework at strategic junctures in the timeline. Organic coherence occurs when the love story is placed at revealing and pivotal plot points.

There's also the balancing act of revealing overarching concepts at critical junctures throughout the plot, encompassing themes such as love, betrayal, and redemption. When combined with masterful pacing, meticulous depth, and lasting intellectual stimulation, these concepts evoke a profound emotional reaction.

A plot in a historical love story involves configuring various storytelling components. It carefully balances pacing with depth, which results in a lasting impact on readers.

# Exploring Themes: Love, Betrayal, and Redemption

The themes of love, betrayal, and redemption create an overwhelming base for the development of historical romance because they provide ample opportunities for story development and resonance for the readers. These themes have existed for centuries, permitting Barbara Cartland and many other authors to wrestle with the intricacies of human emotion, relationships, and societal constructs engagingly and persuasively. Without a doubt, love stands out as one of the major rallying points of most historical romances. It comes in many forms – unrequited love, forbidden love, devotion, selfless love, among others. Cartland's historical romances highlight love, embodying its diverse sides, including the joy of falling in love and the anguish of heartbreak. With the exploration of love in these romance novels, readers will have a greater understanding of how to nurture and cultivate empathy for the extreme nuances of human relationships. To Cartland's narratives, betrayal widens the arc of depth by encompassing conflict and moral grey areas that often challenge one's beliefs, allegiances, and loyalties. In one way through acts of betrayal or poignant revelations of trust betrayed, betrayal evokes timeless romances with riveting tension, adding drama and surprise that draws people toward and changes the outcome to solve a new twist.

Moreover, redemption allows for self-improvement, forgiveness and emotional cleansing. Cartland skillfully traverses through the maze of redemption, depicting the protagonists' journeys towards self-forgiveness and societal acceptance with profound gentleness. Focusing on human frailty and resilience, redemption transforms historical romances from banal fiction into stories that imprint hope and catharsis onto readers. Redefining hope, catharsis and romance through these themes deeply grounded within humanity's struggles, Cartland and her contemporaries escape the simplistic definition of women authors writing love stories, crafting complex romances that appeal to our intellect and deeper emotions while changing the fabric of literature.

# Cultural Impact: The Enduring Appeal of Romantic Narratives

Romantic narratives have emerged from cultures worldwide for centuries and have had a widespread impact. Striking tales of love, heartbreak and reconciliation have shaped almost every domain, be it literature, cinema, or even the world of entertainment. Bestselling books and timeless classics capture readers' attention because of the emotions presented, appealing to people across multiple regions.

Romantic narratives provide insight into different historical settings. Whether they capture the grandeur of England's Regency-era ballrooms or detail love set against the backdrop of war-torn landscapes, these narratives focus on human relationships and the complex phenomenon of love. They explore deeply ingrained themes such as sacrifice, passion, and perseverance, providing readers with a window into the human condition, eager for reflection and self-exploration of their beliefs about love.

Romantic narratives have a broad and extensive impact through literature and other artistic mediums. Compelling stories of sorrow and victory brought to life in the visual arts through theatre and film tell profound and relatable tales. Moreover, sound and music have a great effect of blending emotion with romance while also evocatively impacting the audience.

Apart from the aforementioned facets of romance, popular culture frequently uses romantic narratives. Themes of star-crossed lovers and forbidden romances that portray heartwarming and sometimes heartbreaking love tend to garner audiences' attention.

These motifs highlight the waning yet longstanding fascination with love that is timeless. This serves as a fountainhead that substantiates the unparalleled leverage romantic narratives hold in forming views about love and human interaction in society.

Romance stories influence the breakdown of traditional boundaries and the promotion of inclusiveness. These narratives have adapted to foster a broader depiction of love and relationships by including a variety of protagonists and themes of empowerment and agency. In doing so, they have encouraged readers to shift toward a more accepting view of love devoid of outdated stereotypes and restrictions.

The most captivating aspect of romance narratives is their transforming nature while simultaneously serving as an important reminder of extraordinary human emotions and experiences. These narratives are constantly changing and adjusting to modern-day culture, and regardless of how they adapt, their impact will be profound, redefining them as timeless pieces of literature and culture.

# Beyond the Pen

## CARTLAND'S INFLUENCE AND ADVOCACY

### Literary Reach: Expanding the Romance Genre

The works of Barbara Cartland turned a wide span of public and romantic fiction towards literature in the 20th Century. She went beyond the elementary boundaries of telling a romance story by including adventurism, history, and social critique. Strongly defined lead female characters set in vividly described historical places helped to overcome the clichés of the genre, thus beginning a new wave of romantic fiction. Cartland's works also published romance, suspense, intrigue, and empowerment, which made a diversified audience read her novels irrespective of nationality or country. Her vibrant characters always appealed to vivid and relatable audiences, thus captivating numerous readers from endless social layers and classes. Cartland's impact on the development of the romance genre is now inspiring countless modern authors and readers, maintaining relevance while challenging the sacred impact she made through vibrant fiction.

# Cultural Impact: Shaping 20th Century Literature

The literature of Barbara Cartland has had a transformative global cultural influence throughout the 20th Century. Her literary works have left an indelible mark on the world of literature. Not only her readers, but the entire literary world and ethos of that period was significantly influenced owing to Cartland's ability to spin enthralling stories that captured the heart of romance and passion. Themes such as love, honour, chivalry; an ideal world where one could escape to and where imaginations could be fulfilled, and where one's dreams were realised and not hindered by numerous hurdles, as described by Cartland in her novels. Her influence waned even during the period when romantic fiction was thought to be static. Throughout history and during her travels, Cartland's works brought into 20th-century literature a sense of glamour and escapism which had been missing for a long time. Romance was a genre that was looked down upon by literary society, but thanks to Cartland's sensitivity and relationship dynamics, it finally earned such recognition within literature. The literary work of Cartland deeply shaped 20th-century literature around the globe. She impacted every corner of the planet with her literature and opened up borders between countries for different cultures and people.

Through tales of love and unwavering strength, Cartland bolstered a global literary culture which praised the human spirit and the absolute power of love. Her unwavering devotion to storytelling and her enormous body of work advanced the realm of 20th-century literature, kindling a revival of romantic passion that still exists in today's literary world. Cartland's cultural influence echoed throughout 20th-century literature, carving out a legacy that remains today.

## Women's Empowerment Through Fiction

The novels of Barbara Cartland stand as a prominent example of groundbreaking fiction that galvanised women's empowerment. The focal point of the stories was women, a theme that was quite unprecedented at the time, and featured characters who actively and resolutely sought to escape the bounds of a constraining society. With her works manifesting heroines who overcame challenges and found self-fulfilment, many women began to change their perspectives about their lives engulfed in a patriarchal society due to the endless possibilities envisioned by Cartland's narratives.

The stories of Cartland demonstrated the strength and resilience of women, revealing not only their capability of facing challenges, but also their ability to take control of their lives. This depiction was critical in challenging the accepted boundaries of gender roles as it sought to give readers a sense of freedom and control over their lives. At a time when women's voices often remained muted, they found affirmation, empowerment, and hope, thanks to the narratives and stories told by Cartland.

Moreover, Cartland's novels equally powerfully portrayed romance and love as traits that strengthened women. She depicted love and its power as an essential trait that transforms people to chase their dreams and escalates them toward their goals. In her stories, Cartland lifted love as something that can and should be pursued because of its power to help women escape the shackles of society and their lives and transform them positively.

Furthermore, Cartland's fervent advocacy for women's social inequities and progression was not limited to her works of fiction. She actively campaigned for equal opportunities for women in all social aspects, including education and health care, working toward the improvement of women's lives in society. Her efforts toward improving the status of women and their rights shaped society and motivated people to fight for a better world.

Essentially, Cartland's depiction of women's fiction empowerment goes past the boundaries of a novel to be considered the embodiment of a visionary appeal which implores readers to rethink the notions of gender, appreciate themselves, and fight for a reality where women would be able to unlock their full potential.

Cartland's legacy is that as enduring modern audiences increasingly recognise the relevance of her work, it proves the ability of literature to reshape the narrative of women's empowered lives.

## Social Advocacy: Bridging Literature and Philanthropy

Cartland's influence is not limited to literature; she actively supported several philanthropic initiatives. During her life, Cartland tried to use her literary influence socially for the good, and she accomplished that by integrating philanthropy with literature. For instance, she supported women's education and health care initiatives, and she was a vocal advocate for poverty alleviation and the arts. Awareness of the barreling social change she could influence made romantic novelist Cartland become a socially responsible writer with all her novels.

One of the focuses of her advocacy work was women and their rights. Her novels brandished strong and independent female protagonists who encouraged readers to overcome adversities to foster a spirit of empowerment within themselves. For instance, in her novels, she often depicted women fighting for their right to education and their right to choose their own path in life. With this, she was able to entertain the readers and leave them with a notion of a developing muse for many women's movements to come. This was possible because Cartland wielded the power to change people's thoughts about gender and 'la femme' through well-crafted fiction.

Cartland actively participated in social welfare causes and used her influence to support many humanitarian programmes beyond themed storytelling. Her work included healthcare, education, poverty, and the arts. Understanding fully the impact of her words, Cartland used her resources to effect change, substantiating that literature is not mere entertainment but a way to elevate human consciousness.

Cartland's robust defence of social and economic policy issues indicates that she understood the roles that literature and philanthropy play in one another. Cartland advocated social issues extensively, portraying progress through social storytelling, which fostered action among her readers. Cartland conveyed This relationship between charity and literature her whole life, defining her legacy as an author dedicated to social change. While contemporary writers and philanthropists continue to benefit from Cartland's advocacy of literature, her impact is still felt through creative platforms. In this regard, the legacy of Barbara Cartland's social advocacy illustrates the power of artistic expression towards humanitarian efforts. It reminds us that fiction, though often imagined, can elicit real change.

## Influence on Contemporary Authors and

## Genres

The effects of Barbara Cartland on contemporary authors and genres are extensive. Her commitment to the romance genre alone has shaped and motivated several authors in contemporary times, not only influencing the prospects of literary history. Cartland's 'sweeping' writing style, rich in history and overly romantic, has inspired many writers who wish to weave intricate tales of love and passion intertwined with adventure. She positively affected works beyond romance, guiding an assortment of literary pieces in unexplored manners. Contemporary writers have inherited Cartland's legacy by romanticising their narratives and embedding Cartland's authentic allure, thus allowing romance fiction to live on. Undeniably, the domains of historical fiction, fantasy, and even science fiction draw varied glimpses of Cartland's influence from the tapestry of her multifaceted narrative skills. Beyond narrative techniques, her influence spans thematic boundaries, as the focus on love, empowerment, and unwavering resilience has inspired countless writings across diverse contemporary genres.

The universal themes she championed have inspired writers to infuse their modern novels with timeless ideals, ensuring that *Cartland's spirit continues to live on through the pages of many novels.* Moreover, Cartland's impact on contemporary authors goes beyond the craft of writing. The foremost issues concerning women and Cartland's advocacy for social change and philanthropy have *inspired many contemporary writers who want to make a difference through their work.* As a result, today's literary landscape continues to embrace and expand upon Cartland's passionately cultivated legacy, which articulately demonstrates her enduring impact. As for the contemporary authors and genres, Cartland's mark is evident in the vision, invention, and, most importantly, the relentless embrace of the profound and all-encompassing nature of love and storytelling.

## Global Readership: Cartland's International Appeal

The impact of Barbara Cartland's literary work is not only confined to the boundaries of her native England. She has captured readers' hearts from different parts of the world through her timeless love tales, which resonate with people from different cultures and languages. As her career progressed, Cartland's works were translated into many languages, enabling her stories to reach readers in countries across continents. Her novels were adored internationally because they encompassed love, hope, and optimism themes. Furthermore, Cartland's ability to give readers an enticing sense of escape through her writing gained her a loyal following worldwide. Her passionate readers became part of a growing global community, ready to experience her new masterpiece with every release. She was admired in English-speaking countries and distant lands where her works were available in translation. Through her captivating tales and unwavering devotion to uplifting narratives,

Cartland was able to unite readers from all over the world.

Barbara Cartland's legend lives on, providing comfort and joy to both new and lifelong readers of her captivating stories. Her enduring presence as a symbol of romance and literature is a testament to the profound emotional impact her work has had on readers worldwide.

## Humanitarian Efforts Beyond Writing

Barbara Cartland was also known for some philanthropic activities, which impacted society significantly along with her literary work. Cartland was dedicated to pursuing charitable work alongside social welfare, giving her a reputation as someone who wanted to create an impact. Whether aiding poverty or advancements in healthcare, the reasons behind her charitable causes stemmed from a deep place regarding the betterment of life for others. She strongly fought against the discrimination of such communities, in which their inclusion or empowerment was simply not an option. How Cartland approached humanitarian activities was greatly fuelled by the need for hope and care and a great leap forward to build a positive society, which she achieved through philanthropy. Understanding how vital education is, she started many projects to provide schooling to underprivileged children, ensuring a better tomorrow for several generations.

Moreover, her strong commitment to endorsing health and

well-being resulted in the construction of medical clinics and other outreach programmes that benefit innumerable people today. Cartland's tireless efforts towards preserving nature demonstrated her all-embracing concern for society, which included the expectation of healthy interaction between humans and the ecosystem. Her activities aimed to maintain ecological balance and protect natural resources for posterity, which showed great wisdom about how to care for the planet. Through her unrelenting advocacy, Cartland motivated people to protect the land, flowers, trees, and animals, bestowing humanity the tremendous gift of guardianship of nature.

Her efforts to foster cultural understanding appealed to global citizens and advanced international friendship and collaboration. Through her standing as a popular novelist and woman of note, Cartland mobilised support and drew attention to issues she deemed humanitarian, demonstrating emphatic compassion, which deserves to be remembered. These charitable acts by Barbara Cartland are monumental acts that depict her philanthropic spirit and ardent wish for a fairer world for all.

## Environmental Concerns and Cartland's Vision

Consequently, Barbara Cartland was unwilling to forgo her literary interests at the expense of the environment. She clearly understood that mankind was dependent on nature and, for that reason, advocated for a change of lifestyle and conservation in her books.

Outside of writing her romance novels, Cartland was an avid advocate for the environment, regularly highlighting the need to protect natural resources and the world for future generations. She did not only talk about such things; she did them. Her efforts in promoting reforestation and supporting the preservation of wildlife helped Cartland maintain the world's ecological balance. In a wider sense, her environmentalism included everything tangible: people's relationship with nature, the emotions it evokes, and the spirit entwined with it. Through her writings, speeches, and public appearances, she tried to cultivate a shared sense of environmental responsibility and care for nature among the public.

Additionally, she strongly advocated for literature as a means of arousing readers' environmental consciousness, regularly intertwining themes of ecological balance and reverence for the natural world in her love stories. The impact of her concern for the environment has, for many readers and admirers, been an inspiration and, at times, a catalyst for activism. Her influence extends beyond fiction, shaping real practices and policies intended to protect the environment. She is a legacy to every modern activist and organisations that need to sustain and nurture the Earth. The unapologetic and enduring essence of Cartland's environmental ideals shows the extent of her influence, beyond fiction, on real practices and policies intended to protect the environment.

# Awards and Recognitions: Acknowledging Contributions

All of Barbra Cartland's works in literature, charity and advocacy have earned her many awards and honours throughout her lifetime. Being the bestselling author that she is, she has received international commendations from literary, cultural and even humanitarian institutions. These awards include [specific awards], proving Cartland's grand impact on society and how her legacy is remembered. The awards Cartland belongs to have established her as a leading figure in the literary world, having received some of the highest accolades in her field due to her unparalleled ability to tell and retell captivating romance stories embraced by people across generations.

Her dedication to maintaining the core elements of romance while simultaneously pushing societal boundaries has firmly established her as an important figure in this genre.

Moreover, she published works that have endured for decades and continue motivating and entertaining readers from around the globe. Besides being an author, Cartland's active participation in other philanthropic endeavours has made her known to several charitable and humanitarian institutions. The initiatives to foster women's rights, women's health, and preservation of nature have positively transformed numerous lives. The International Women's Day Honoree and the Humanitarian Excellence Award are examples of accolades affirming her continuous advocacy for the constructive development of people and communities worldwide. Moreover, her remarkable literary works campaigning for social causes have earned her honorary degrees and fellowships from reputable colleges and universities. She has advanced the advocacy of social issues such as equal rights for women, education for all, and care for the environment through her literary works that tackle real-life problems. Also, Cartland has been recognised for her contribution to modern authors and genres, and honours have been bestowed on her for motivating contemporary romance fiction writers. The Pink Heart Award, named after her, recognises exceptional achievements in romance writing, which she deemed as a genre that embodies her aspirations of love, compassion and hope.

This award epitomises Cartland's eternal mark while inspiring future writers to continue her tradition of promoting love and empowerment. Her numerous accolades testify to her enduring impact on literature, social advancement, and humanity as a whole. To conclude, Barbara Cartland received numerous honours that serve as milestones for her extraordinary achievements and unwavering dedication to nurturing the literary world and catalysing social transformation.

# Cartland's Enduring Influence Today

Cartland's legacy is of monumental importance to the literary sphere and the world as she fundamentally reshaped the understanding of romance, literature, and social advocacy. Her remarkable works span continents and generations, establishing her as an everlasting icon of women's empowerment. The sustained publication of her books, alongside their global allure, proves her timeless influence. Cartland's strong advocacy for love, bravery, and independence in her characters continues to appeal to modern society, showcasing the timelessness of her narratives. In addition to her advocacy for women, her revolutionary methods of depicting characters and stories set a benchmark for upcoming writers and continue to ignite passion in authors of the romance genre and beyond.

Aside from her writing, Cartland's advocacy of philanthropic and humanitarian actions inspires many who wish to change the world. Her active participation in and championing of women's causes, her initiative in charitable projects, and her work towards the conservation of the environment exemplify the scope of her influence.

Hers was a self-crafted culture that integrated fashion and contemporary art, making her a timeless icon. Many know her novels, but not all recognise her lasting impact on society and culture. The awards and honourees established after her prove her immeasurable influence. Take, for example, the award tailored to recognise achievements in romance literature bearing her name, the Barbara Cartland Pink Biblio Award, honouring authors who capture the spirit of romantic literature that Cartland proudly pioneered. Her impacts are widespread, as evident with her romantic literature awards and accompanying recognition. To sum up, she actively engaged with every modern societal and daughter issue. Even schooled them in her book, cementing her role as the vanguard of romance, advocacy, and remarkable literature.

# Pink Perfection

## CULTIVATING AN ENCHANTING PUBLIC PERSONA

## The Origin of the Pink Aesthetic

Her philosophy and public image heavily shaped Barbara Cartland's love for pink, which later became her signature aesthetic. The connection between Cartland and pink can be traced back to her belief in the power of positivity, romanticism, and unconditional timelessness adorning the world around us. It is common knowledge that Barbara Cartland developed a strong fondness for pink from a very early age. Her family's gardens featured soft pink roses, which, during her formative years, made a strong imprint in her psyche. This infatuation with the colour eventually culminated in recognising the impact and effect pink had on her peaceful state, which she desperately sought to emulate and propagate worldwide. Upon entering society's bow, Cartland used this opportunity to turn her trademark into a brand, using pink to showcase her oversized persona. She understood that the colour pink's association with femininity, grace and gentleness encapsulated her values, aspirations and public image. Henceforth, pink could no longer be perceived merely as a colour; it had merged with her identity, manifesting her beliefs and ideals.

Barbara Cartland effectively utilised pink in all of her public appearances, photographs, and written literature to create a trademark aesthetic throughout her career. The image she sculpted using her decorations and clothes was simple and instantly recognisable to the public. The pink aesthetic was critical to Cartland's legacy; it represented the romantic charm and enchanting allure of her works and public image. Eventually, pink transformed from being just a favorite color into a declaration of fidelity to optimism, love, and beauty. This ensures that Barbara Cartland's legacy, always associated with the allure of pink, will be remembered and appreciated for generations to come.

# Public Appearances: Creating a Timeless Image

Cartland's public appearances served as a meticulous widespread celebration, crafted with care, to tend to her enchanting public persona. Through her stunning drama, no one could deny the charm with which she infused every public appearance. Romance wafted in her presence during events ranging from book launches to charity galas and even to literary festivals that she attended.

Those fortunate enough to come across her were always spellbound. Furthermore, every single aspect she executed meticulously reinforced her lingering image, hence, every grin, each pronunciation, and movement cascaded forth with flawless precision beyond clothing selection. Her sophisticated and ever so captivated appeal across multiple spectacles wields timeless influence and renowned status as a woman transcending boundaries of literature and social interaction. Most notably, enduring charming appeal without being overly delicate shaped perceptions of countless generations ~ effortless anticipation. Every public engagement across the globe and her image evolved through her appeal of romance in reality and fiction glamourised notions of love. Public engagements transformed into an illusion where one simplistic reality was advocated as a relentless proclamation that shaped romanticism - and love, crafting an elusion Cartland wielded on her audience, captivating them with her enduring charm.

At these events, she effortlessly integrated her persona with her career and strengthened the symbiotic relationship of both her personal and professional brands. Through her public appearances, Cartland both sold her books and served as an expository illustration of the principles and values she advanced and distorted in her novels. In doing so, she wove herself into a dazzling figure of the ethereal world she created in her novels, wowing everyone with her warmth and otherworldly charm. With her stunning fashion choices and sophisticated persona, Cartland turned every public appearance into a timeless opportunity to assert her claim as the pinnacle of romance, making these her moments to 'shine.' She showed people her relentless approach to sandwiching perfection as she approached writing. Thus, her shared image remains as flawless and timeless as it was in her prime, which shows a testament to her enduring skill at branding.

## Media Savvy: Navigating Interviews and Press Interactions

Understanding the media's potential to influence public image, Barbara Cartland engaged in interviews and interactions with the utmost skill. She approached the press with storytelling in mind, which was a powerful tool in her attempt to dazzle audiences and capture their attention. Mix and mingle, Cartland did with the interviews and other publicity opportunities, so her entertainment persona was always 'on brand' and charming. While conveying elegance, femininity, and devotion to her craft, eloquence on her part allowed for the astute interpretation of her audience's perceptions. Moreover, Cartland's media savvy deflection of invasive questions in favour of her literary works ensured her audience remembered her as such. Charm and poise became her mainstay claim, and with them, Barb became known as the media—and readers'—fascinating chronicler of unforgettable impressions. Many of her fans knew little about the timing of the various media bursts her multi-faceted persona would tumble out of. Still, Cartland always managed to retain her captivating obsessiveness and sophisticated relevance. As a literary darling of the press, Barb had long secured her title as a popular romance author and global culture figure.

Cartland utilised her captivating personality and devoted herself to a singular story, which enabled her to achieve an incredible feat: an aura of mystery that bordered on the supernatural. As a result, she forged a lasting impact in the world of books and show business.

## Fashion as a Signature: Cartland's Wardrobe Selections

Barbara Cartland's wardrobe choices were not simply a case of personal inclination; they formed an aspect of her cultivated self. Known for her love of all things pink, Cartland painstakingly developed a signature style she was known for since it was recognisable to her audience. Her clothing radiated grace and womanliness, aligned with the romantic spirit that surrounded her writing. Wearing pastel pinks was common for Cartland, bringing forth an image of timelessness. In addition to these, her clothes had a heavy and extravagant style, often decorated in lace, pearls, and richly embroidered fabric. These components came together with sophisticated charm, resembling the imagery in her novels. But it was not just about personal style; Cartland's fashion choices were a strategic marketing tool, reinforcing her image as an author of romance novels. Every ensemble was strategically styled to perpetuate the mystical charm she cultivated, and her book cover designs and advertising also featured her signature design, promoting uniformity and brand cohesion.

The strategic blend of her personal style and professional branding strengthened her image with her readers and the public, cementing her impact as a noted literary figure. Ultimately, Cartland used fashion to captivate her audience by incorporating charm and steadfast grace into all her public undertakings.

# Iconic Branding: From Book Covers to Personal Style

Barbara Cartland's brilliant self-branding included all her public activities and self-presentation, such as book covers and style. She was successful as a romance writer and figure of culture due to her distinct branding as a romance author. The covers of her books were wrought with romantic artwork containing a recognisable picture combined with her signature Cartland hand lettering of sequels. This meticulous attention to detail was mainly focused on presenting her novels, and their portrayal spelt out captivating promises of romance and timeless beauty.

Cartland's styling preferences were as much a part of this marketing plan as anything else, as she donned chiaroscuro-dreamlike and richly decorated gowns outfitted with laces that emulated the fairy tale world she so vividly painted in her books. The dresses and skirts adorned with laces, ribbons and flowers she put on were direct examples of the luxury and ostentation she so lovingly described in exile in her novels. Her turn towards a disguise that reflected part of her novel's fantasy lands enabled Cartland to guide her fans through her books and her life full of magic and charm.

She paid the same attention to her public appearances, where she made sure to sit with her head held high and exuded grace, poise, charm, and, most importantly, approachability.

Whether attending book signings, speaking engagements, or social functions, she meticulously planned every detail to project an image of romance, sophistication, and timeless charm that her brand epitomised. With her outfits and composure, she radiated unapologetic femininity, captivating and charming the audiences while embodying her romantic novels.

This blend of literature with personal branding enabled her to transcend the status of an author and become an enduring icon of romance and elegance. Cartland's branded self-image not only represented her but also shaped the entire perception of romance literature, elevating it from the world of litcrature to a realm of wealth, fantasy, and aspiration to ensnaring worlds. Thus, Barbara Cartland became an everlasting symbol of romance, an enduring icon of timeless grace and enchantment, and forged her legacy as more than just a writer.

# The Role of Humour and Wit in Persona Building

The establishment and maintenance of a public persona are integral to the enduring legacy of Barbara Cartland. Amidst her iconic branding, one cannot overlook the pivotal role of humour and wit in cultivating an enchanting public image that continues to captivate audiences. Cartland's remarkable ability to infuse her interactions with a lighthearted and engaging charm has left an indelible mark on her persona. She created an aura of approachability and warmth through her clever use of humour, endearing herself to countless fans. Whether engaging in interviews, public appearances, or addressing her readership, Cartland leveraged humour as a foundation for connection, effectively inviting individuals into her whimsical world. This strategic incorporation of wit reinforced her brand and fostered a sense of intimacy and rapport with her audience. Further enhancing her persona, her quick-wittedness and sardonic humour were instrumental in navigating through challenging or controversial topics, often deftly deflecting criticism while maintaining grace and elegance. Remarkably, this facet of Cartland's persona contributed to the transcendence of her literary persona into a relatable, beloved figure for her admirers.

By embracing humour as a cornerstone of her public image, Cartland demonstrated a keen understanding of the power of levity in forging enduring connections.

Furthermore, her playful banter and humorous anecdotes during public readings and signings endeared her to fans, fostering a sense of shared joy and camaraderie. This allowed her admirers to have intimate glimpses into the wit that fueled her artistry, enriching their experience of her works. It is evident that humour and wit not only served as an indispensable tool for character-building but also lent an irresistible charm to Cartland's interactions with her audience. Even beyond her literary endeavours, Cartland's embodiment of humour and wit extended to her public persona, affirming her status as a timeless cultural icon whose influence transcends generations. In sum, the judicious application of humour and wit remains a defining attribute in the perennial appeal of Barbara Cartland, reaffirming her as an exemplary paradigm for persona-building and connecting with audiences in the realm of literature and beyond.

# Engaging with Fans: Signings and Public Readings

Engaging directly with readers through book signings and public readings remains integral to Barbara Cartland's enchanting public persona. These in-person interactions provide a unique opportunity for her to connect with her loyal fanbase, offering a glimpse into the creative process while fostering a sense of community and appreciation. Cartland greeted her admirers with warmth and grace at book signings, taking the time to chat with each individual and personalize their copies with heartfelt messages. Her genuine interest in her readers and their experiences further endeared her to a devoted audience, solidifying the emotional bond between author and fan. These interactions showcased her approachable nature and added a personal touch to her literary legacy, creating cherished keepsakes for her supporters. Public readings offered another avenue for Cartland to engage with her fans, captivating audiences with her eloquence and theatrical flair. Whether reciting passages from her latest works or sharing anecdotes from her storied career, she skillfully brought her narratives to life, leaving a lasting impression on all in attendance. Her ability to transport listeners to the enchanting worlds she crafted within her novels elevated these events beyond mere promotional efforts, elevating them into unforgettable experiences for her dedicated followers.

Furthermore, these engagements served as platforms for Cartland to inspire and mentor aspiring writers, imparting wisdom and encouragement to those eager to pursue their literary dreams. Her generosity in sharing her knowledge and experiences exemplified her commitment to nurturing talent and supporting the next generation of storytellers, fostering a legacy far beyond her celebrated body of work. Through her participation in signings and public readings, Barbara Cartland engaged with her fans on a personal level. She perpetuated the magic of storytelling, leaving an indelible mark on the hearts and minds of countless enthusiasts.

These events, characterized by warmth, elegance, and mutual appreciation, stand as enduring testaments to her influence and the power of human connection in the literary world.

# The Power of Consistency: Predictability as an Asset

Consistency is the hallmark of enduring success in the literary world, and Barbara Cartland deftly harnessed its power to solidify her position as a beloved figure in readers' hearts. The reliability of her enchanting narratives and the consistency of her public persona worked in harmony to create an aura of trustworthiness and reliability. Cartland effectively created a brand synonymous with romance and elegance by maintaining a consistent style, tone, and thematic approach throughout her prolific career. One of the key aspects of consistency in Cartland's work was the predictability of her storytelling. Her audience came to expect certain elements in every novel – a dashing hero, a captivating heroine, sumptuous historical settings, and ultimately, a happily-ever-after conclusion. This predictability was not a limitation but rather a cornerstone of her success, for it allowed readers to immerse themselves in a world where they could anticipate a satisfying resolution and indulgent escapism. In embracing this consistency, Cartland demonstrated a profound understanding of her audience's desires and leveraged it to build a loyal readership. Beyond her literary endeavours, Cartland also exhibited consistency in her public appearances and interactions. From her distinct attire to her unwavering dedication to engaging with fans, she projected an image of stability and dependability. This steadfastness engendered an enduring connection with her audience, many of whom cherished the familiarity inherent in her public persona. Cartland's consistency provided a comforting anchor in an ever-changing world, allowing her admirers to rely on her enduring presence in literature and public life. Moreover, the power of consistency extended into the marketing and promotion of her works. Publishers and readers alike knew what to expect from a Barbara Cartland novel, and this predictability facilitated the ongoing success of her releases. The unwavering nature of her brand meant that readers could confidently anticipate a new tale of romance and glamour. At the same time, publishers could depend on reliable sales figures and dedicated fan engagement. Consequently, Cartland's consistency became an asset in enriching her literary creations and sustaining her commercial viability over the years. In essence, the power of consistency served as a guiding principle for Barbara Cartland, allowing her to cultivate an enduring legacy rooted in unwavering reliability and predictable charm. It shaped her literary output and defined the essence of her public persona, establishing her as an icon of consistency and dependability in an evolving world.

## Maintaining Enchantment: Adapting to Changing Times

Societal norms, cultural expectations, and literary preferences undergo substantial transformations over time. As an iconic figure in romance literature, Barbara Cartland recognized the significance of evolving with the times while preserving the enchanting essence that defined her persona and work. Adapting to changing times was not merely a response to external pressures but a strategic decision rooted in Cartland's innate ability to understand and connect with her audience. Through astute observation and meticulous analysis, she identified shifts in societal ideals and aspirations, tailoring her narratives to reflect the evolving desires of her readership. Embracing new themes, nuanced characterizations, and contemporary settings became integral to ensuring that Cartland's novels remained relevant and captivating. The author adeptly infused her timeless romantic tropes with modern sensibilities, offering a seamless blend of tradition and innovation that resonated deeply with her audience. In addition to literary adaptations, Cartland recognized the importance of engaging through various media platforms to sustain her allure amidst changing communication landscapes. Leveraging emerging technologies and media channels, she expanded her reach and interacted with readers in ways that were reflective of contemporary society. By embracing radio, television, and eventually digital media, Cartland extended the enchantment of her persona beyond the realm of literature, solidifying her status as an enduring cultural icon. While navigating shifting paradigms, Cartland remained steadfast in her commitment to empowering her readers with tales of enduring love, unwavering optimism, and unyielding strength. Her ability to seamlessly adapt to changing times without compromising her core values exemplifies a rare balance of flexibility and unwavering authenticity, creating a legacy that transcends generations. As the world continues to evolve, the enchantment of Barbara Cartland's work serves as an evergreen testament to the timeless power of love, connection, and resilience, reminding us all that adapting to change does not dilute the essence of enchantment but rather amplifies its everlasting impact.

# Critics vs. Admirers: Managing Public Perception

Navigating the complex landscape of public perception is a recurring challenge for any public figure, and Barbara Cartland was no exception. As an iconic figure in the literary world, she garnered a broad spectrum of opinions from critics and admirers alike. The delicate balance between managing these differing views while maintaining authenticity and integrity was a nuanced art form that Cartland mastered throughout her career. For every fervent admirer captivated by her enchanting narratives and timeless romance, there existed a critic ready to scrutinize and dissect her work. Cartland's ability to navigate this contrasting spectrum with grace and astuteness was a testament to her resilience and unwavering commitment to her craft. Instead of engaging in contentious debates or confrontations, she focused on her dedicated readership and stayed true to her storytelling prowess. In the realm of managing public perception, Cartland was keenly aware of the power of constructive criticism. Rather than dismissing critiques outright, she conscientiously evaluated feedback, using it as a catalyst for growth and refinement. This approach earned her respect within literary circles and demonstrated her humility and willingness to evolve as a writer. By addressing criticisms thoughtfully, Cartland showcased her professionalism and dedication to her stories and audience.

Furthermore, Cartland's adept public perception management extended beyond her literary works. Her public image, carefully cultivated over the years, required meticulous attention to detail. With a flair for fashion and an innate understanding of branding, she presented herself as a captivating embodiment of her romantic narratives. By embracing her persona as an extension of her craft, she fostered a sense of enchantment that resonated with her admirers, ultimately overshadowing the detractors. Cartland's strategic approach to managing public perception also involved actively engaging with her audience. She ensured that her admirers felt valued and appreciated through public appearances, book signings, and personal interactions. This genuine connection with her readers built a loyal following that bolstered her reputation against critical voices. Her ability to cultivate a community around her work contributed significantly to her enduring legacy as a beloved romance novelist.

In conclusion, managing public perception is a multifaceted endeavour that demands careful navigation and calculated responses. Barbara Cartland's adeptness in negotiating the dichotomy between critics and admirers is a paragon of effective public relations. Her ability to maintain grace, humility, and empathy in the face of scrutiny solidified her position as an esteemed figure in literature, leaving an indelible mark on the hearts and minds of her devoted readers.

# Royal Connections

## GUIDING THE PRINCESS OF WALES

### A Fateful Meeting: Cartland and the Royal Family

The British Royal Family's first encounter with Cartland marked the beginning of the influence she wielded over the family, especially while guiding the younger members. It was an incident of tremendous importance that would permanently affect her life and career. From her first encounters with the Royals, Cartland seemed to possess an uncanny ability to engage with nobles, as she could win their affection and admiration through her charm, intellect, and broad life experiences. This ability to deal with the aristocracy would later help her form her distinct relationship with the Princess of Wales, ultimately shaping her legacy. The first meeting with the Royal Family wasn't merely a meet-and-greet; it was the starting point for a redefined Cartland that would have an impact beyond the borders of literature. As private glimpses behind palaces and castle curtains became normalised for Cartland, so did her integration into the circles of power and privilege.

Her skill in managing this sphere with composure and dignity won her the royal family's affection, allowing her to offer her guidance and mentorship to highly public figures. From this chance encounter, Cartland found herself at the point where history met modernity, solidifying her position as a confidante and advisor to auras whose lives were, in essence, far removed from the daily lives of her readers. It was in these regal confines that Cartland realised a new vocation—one that went beyond her writing and involved the gentle shaping of young hearts and minds tempered by royal privileges. More than a series of happenstances and deliberate decisions began to unite a tale of love and admiration between Cartland and the Royal Family, building the foundation for the mentorship that would blossom in later years.

## Mentorship Blossoms: Establishing a Unique Bond

The development of Barbara Cartland's relationship with the Princess of Wales is a remarkable example of an archetypal mentorship. Initially, their relationship was founded on mutual admiration for traditions and grace. Over time, it transformed into an unbreakable bond forged through shared principles, empathy, and deeper understanding. The Princess's transformation under Cartland's mentorship is a testament to the power of guidance and influence, inspiring all who witness it.

Outside the boundaries of proper etiquette and royal decorum, Cartland and the Princess shared a thrilling bond formed out of empathy and concern for each other's welfare. Through incisive discussions and moments of vulnerability, they cultivated a connection that transcended their divergent social levels, resulting in a partnership based on trust and authenticity.

Cartland's steadfast resolve in steering the young Princess through the complexities of her public persona was a significant characterising aspect of their mentorship. With poise and diplomacy, she taught her age-old yet timeless lessons on diplomacy, decorum, and the public-private identity nexus. Such lessons, coloured by Cartland's experience with societal expectations, profoundly impacted the way the Princess embraced her royal duties.

Furthermore, Cartland's willingness to be mentored by the Princess revealed how the former admired the latter's ability to blend custom and innovation while imbuing the royal family with a traditionally modern sense of confidence and fortitude. Through Cartland's lessons, the Princess could embrace the figurative mantle of a new resolve, which enabled her to become a figure of compassion and grace both within and outside the borders of her home country.

Their distinctive bond enhanced personal development and

represented a blend of old-world polish and modern thoughts. It went beyond ordinary mentorship frameworks to depict authentic companionship grounded in profound admiration and common principles. As this connection further developed, it affected the royal milieu, significantly altering the course of the Princess's life and the institution she served. The depth of their relationship is palpable, resonating with the audience.

# Guidance in Grace: Steering Royal Etiquette and Public Perceptions

The scope of Barbara Cartland's mentorship to the Princess of Wales included aiding her in the public's etiquette and perception. Cartland educated her on the intricacies surrounding demeanour, poise, and etiquette, allowing her to adequately manage her royal duties. Having spent decades in high society, Cartland extracted the best societal norms to impose on the Princess to help her maintain regal etiquette and proper bearing. These principles spanned from formal events and diplomatic functions to unanticipated public encounters where Cartland's expectations of composure had fused with the Princess's public life to stamp her royal being. Beyond that, Cartland fully understood the public and media's impact on the monarchy. Aware of perception's influence, she taught the Princess how to construct and project a traditional crown-supporting image to the public. Through private meetings, Cartland sought to make the Princess understand the need for balance between relatability and tradition, emphasising the need for approachability despite a dignified presence.

Cartland's work on shaping the Princess's public relations was not limited to the surface level. She undertook the deeper work of fostering an authentic connection with people. Her lessons of engaged philanthropy, accompanied by empathy and compassion, guided the Princess to connect with different communities of people, which paralleled Cartland's social advocacy throughout her life in the public arena. This form of caring fell outside mere service, leading people to see the Princess as an approachable figure they admired because she genuinely cared about others. The Princess's genuine care for others is a testament to her character, resonating with the audience.

## A Stylist Touch: Influencing Fashion Choices Behind Palace Walls

The impact of Barbara Cartland's influence on fashion selections within royal circles transcended her mere concern with their aesthetics. With her keen eye for grace and etiquette, she wielded considerable power in shaping the sartorial expressions of the upper crust. Cartland appreciated the role of apparel as a nonverbal form of communication because every outfit worn by a royal family member sent a signal to the public and the entire world. She sought to guide fashion decisions behind castle walls with an appreciation for the conventions, albeit with flexibility for contemporary styles and trends. Such thoughtful counsel as she offered would navigate the tricky waters of regal dignity and modernity. So sensitive were her methods that they ensured that the sartorial choices of the Princess of Wales and other leading ladies maintained an aura of elegance, sophistication, and timelessness, courtesy of Cartland's unrivalled expertise in matters of grace. Beyond preference, Cartland's influence on the royal family's fashion choices significantly enhanced their public image, projecting an image of elegance, sophistication, and modernity and forever etching her name in the history of fashion.

Elaborate royal elegance and haute fashion were transformed by her intense focus on detail and demands for high dress standards. By supporting designers who interpreted elegance with the same precision, Cartland carved out her place as a tastemaker to whom high society and popular culture both answered, her influence unmatched. The imprints of her unparalleled discerning eye will not only be remembered as engravings of regal fashion, but they also affirm her undying legacy as a style icon.

## The Social Landscape: Navigating High Society with Finesse

The high society world captivated Barbara Cartland's attention, and she swiftly became a revered figure due to her accurate grasp and elegant manners. Her mastery of social relations went beyond basic etiquette, enabling her to skillfully manage the intricacies of aristocratic relations. Sustaining the customs and traditions of the elite, she effortlessly participated in elite functions as a picture of a svelte aplomb. Propriety, great respect in her circle, and guarded discretion became hallmarks of her reputation. Those skilled in social affairs entrusted her with their charm.

Along with her articulate speech skills, she was able to warm up to the greats and was impressed with her wit. Society always needed Cartland's deft balancing hunches and currents, enhancing her understanding – unrivalled access from within – into the inner circle of high society circles. Moreover, her social adaptability and unspoken protocol compliance proved Cartland's refined adaptability. Being a distinguished guest at others' prestigious events served as evidence of her unyielding status and aroused admiration towards her sophisticated presence that commanded respect.

Cartland was the very definition of graciousness and sophistication from the first meeting, shaping her legacy among those who had the privilege of meeting her. From hosting lavish parties to attending extravagant galas, she perpetually followed the rules of etiquette, securing her reputation as a sophisticated socialite. As much as Cartland amazed high society, she garnered admiration and served as a beacon to those seeking to navigate the formidable waters of aristocratic etiquette and manners. Her intuitive understanding of social hierarchies and diplomatic relationships ensured that she maintained effortless relationships and alliances, further strengthening her dominant position within the upper class of society. Her elegant manner with which she engaged in these circles established a legacy for future generations that encouraged the pursuit of refinement and poise needed as a welcome addition to the tower of high society.

# An Empathetic Ear: Personal Conversations and Shared Wisdom

In upper-class circles, personal conversations, as a distinct form of dialogue, stand out for their carefully nuanced nature, particularly in relation to prominent individuals. The stunning example is set by Barbara Cartland, who managed to hold empathic dialogues with the Princess of Wales. These encounters speak volumes not just about her wisdom, but about understanding people and their social relations in providing shared wisdom. These private conversations were crucial, not simply as social formalities, but served as critical channels for interaction, assistance, and sharing life lessons.

With Cartland's genuine compassion and astute perceptiveness, she reached an emotional depth far greater than that of the ordinary mentor-mentee relationship. Through these discussions, she was able to offer the princess a trusted confidante, someone who knew her face and who understood the unique nature of her role and the constant pressure she endured. Cartland's well-developed impression enabled her to present views and advice relevant to the princess's private life, thus forging a relationship based on respect and understanding.

The insights derived from such dialogues did not only involve common etiquette or public image; they also pertained to professional and social interactions, emotional intelligence, human relationships, and the intricate interplay of one's responsibilities and privileges. Cartland's experiences and wisdom proved instrumental to the princess during their conversations, which further enhanced the princess's understanding of life through literature and social life.

Cartland also offered her services as a sympathetic listener during state occasions and formal functions. Their talks included personal hardships and goals, balancing tradition and modernity, and staying authentic to oneself. It was within these moments that Cartland while nurturing the princess's raw emotions, mentored her to transform her newfound vulnerability into a compassionate source of strength, all while providing sage advice and unwavering support.

In the end, the private exchanges between Barbara Cartland and the Princess of Wales signified more than the transfer of wisdom; they marked knowledge sharing as an everlasting connection that stems from kindness, trust, and mutual perseverance under scrutiny. Their exchanges still resonate today as an example of the strong effects of empathy and the importance of personal, unpretentious relationships in an environment usually characterised by decorum and pretence.

## Public Life Strategies: Coping with Attention from the Media Gracefully

In the world of etiquette and royalty, the media is an ever-present force that must be managed precisely. These were the circumstances under which the Princess of Wales needed guidance from Barbara Cartland. With her extensive knowledge of etiquette, Cartland understood how to help the Princess of Wales during media frenetics. She understood how the need for poise and control, even during press onslaughts of media frenzy, created opportunities to manage media relations.

One of the key strategies championed by Cartland was the practice of selective disclosure. Reasoning that keeping some things private can be just as important as interacting with the press, Cartland provided counsel to the princess regarding how best to manage her public and private life. This cultivated some degree of mystery around her and added to her charm while protecting her sanctity. She also advised the princess on media management strategies.

In addition, Cartland championed using the media as a conduit for charitable work and advocacy. Aligning the princess's public engagements with charitable causes allowed them to garner media coverage for good deeds. This asserted that positive coverage of charitable activities cited as encouraging the princess's publicity would also result in meaningful change.

Furthermore, Cartland paid attention to other forms of expression and physical gestures toward the media. She taught the princess how to use facial and body gestures that emanate grace, confidence, and friendliness. Ingrained in Cartland's principles was the cultivation of beneficial, long-lasting relationships with journalists and media figures. Cartland valued respect and encouraged the princess to foster friendships with significant media personalities, vouching that these friendships would assist in dealing with public opinion, which could be manipulated to showcase the princess in a positive light.

Under Cartland's guidance, the princess managed the media's attention with exceptional grace and poise. Through strategic silence, leveraging the media for charitable causes, effective body language, and cultivating media insiders, the princess was able to present herself as a poised figure during her nonstop public attention. This effective management of the media spotlight is a testament to the power of Cartland's strategies.

## Public Life Strategies: Handling Media Attention with Poise

In the realm of high society and royalty, media attention is a constant presence that demands careful navigation. Barbara Cartland, with her deep understanding of etiquette and public perception, was instrumental in guiding the Princess of Wales through the complex terrain of media scrutiny. Cartland recognized the significance of maintaining composure and grace under the unrelenting gaze of the press, thus emphasizing the importance of strategic interactions with the media.

One of the key strategies advocated by Cartland was the art of selective disclosure. Understanding that maintaining a sense of mystery and privacy can be as impactful as engaging with the media, Cartland advised the princess on delicately balancing public and private life. This deliberate approach fostered an air of intrigue around her, enhancing her allure while safeguarding her personal sanctity.

Furthermore, Cartland espoused the concept of using the media as a vehicle for philanthropic initiatives and advocacy. By strategically aligning the princess's public appearances and engagements with charitable causes, they were able to harness the power of media exposure for the greater good. Cartland's guidance underscored the notion that positive media coverage arising from altruistic endeavors would not only elevate the princess's public image but also contribute to meaningful societal impact.

Additionally, Cartland emphasized the importance of non-verbal communication when facing the media. She coached the princess in the art of body language and facial expressions, recognizing their potential to convey poise, confidence, and warmth. By diligently honing these non-verbal cues, the princess could effectively communicate without uttering a word, demonstrating her grace and dignity even amidst intense media scrutiny.

Cartland's sage advice extended to the cultivation of enduring relationships with reputable journalists and media personalities. Emphasizing the value of respect and mutual understanding, Cartland encouraged the princess to foster amicable associations with influential individuals in the media sphere. These alliances proved invaluable in navigating the often turbulent waters of public opinion and casting the princess in a favorable light.

Ultimately, under Cartland's astute guidance, the princess adeptly handled media attention with an unparalleled degree of poise. By employing strategic discretion, leveraging the media for philanthropic endeavors, mastering non-verbal communication, and nurturing alliances within the media landscape, the princess emerged as a beacon of elegance and grace amidst the relentless glare of public scrutiny.

## Cultural Patronage: Encouraging Philanthropy and Arts Engagement

Barbara Cartland's influence was not limited to literature. It also impacted philanthropy and the arts. Her cultural patronage and philanthropic undertakings revealed her as a compassionate and beauty-loving woman. Cartland believed and made it her business to teach those around her that music, art, and charity were pillars of life that needed to be preserved and cherished.

With an astonishing social presence, charm, and wealth, Cartland donated to numerous charitable projects and worked hard to motivate others, especially people of power, to do the same. As a result of her relentless advocacy and personal efforts, a culture of giving and a supportive environment were created for the arts, allowing many sought-after and talented individuals to nurture and develop.

To stimulate giving, she organised a variety of fundraising activities. Gifted with social connections, she often organised effective campaigns in high society. She executed everything from lavish galas to auctions to private parties with remarkable poise and, most importantly, a lot of determination. She aimed to increase funding for her initiatives, always ensuring her actions made a difference.

Cartland's influence extended beyond her financial support. She championed the creation and preservation of artistic works, recognising their importance to individuals and communities. Her efforts to promote arts education and support artistic institutions have had a profound and lasting impact on society, forever changing countless lives.

Apart from her financial support, Cartland's passionate commitment towards cultivating developing talent and helping more established artists attests to her dedication to deepening engagement with the arts. By offering mentorship, publicity opportunities, and unmatched support, she enabled more than artistry visionaries to transcend boundaries and defy norms, thus sustaining the transformation of artistic expression.

The scope of Cartland's philanthropy and cultural patronage did not include financial aid alone; it was more of an all-encompassing effort to better society by creating conditions for constructive artistic and humanitarian endeavours that are sustainable. Her legacy here still challenges contemporaries in a positive sense, demonstrating how her commitment to philanthropy and the arts is ever-present with urgency. Through boundless commitment, Cartland demonstrated that the irreplaceable symbiosis of creativity and compassion is an everlasting source for a better and enriched world.

# A Controversial Influence: Varied Perspectives on Cartland's Role

The legacy of Barbara Cartland contains a blend of admiration and critique regarding her impact as a mentor to the Princess of Wales. For one, supporters consider her a mentor who provided necessary lessons and teachings to a woman who faced the public's gaze far too early. Hall of Famer Cartland's hallmarks of grace, kindness, and charity are agreeable within royal circles for possessing a positive, timeless nature. Her support for charity and engagement with the arts is pivotal to the princess's advocacy and charitable initiatives.

On the other side, some believe that these aspects of philanthropy and charity need progression and modernity. Others argue that by teaching such principles, Cartland may have hindered the independent development of the princess, thus reinforcing regressive societal norms and expectations around women. Moreover, some have been sceptical towards the perceived claim that Cartland was the all-encompassing reason behind the gateway to new experiences and growth for the princess. As with anything involving deeply rooted traditions, the heated discussions surrounding Cartland's legacy unveil an enduring conflict of a society divided between cherishing established norms and progress and supporting evolution.

Cartland's impact, whether controversial or not, goes beyond speculation as it has affected public opinion and scholarly work. While some individuals appreciate the impact of her mentorship, praising it as important in shaping the image and actions of a beloved figure, others warn us not to idealise the bygone standards and norms of a bygone era. And while these debates continue, we realise that Cartland's legacy goes beyond her romantic novels and entails her deep involvement in the life of a royal figure.

# The Enduring Impact: How Guidance Shaped Future Generations

Barbara Cartland's instruction of the Wales princess has had salient effects on subsequent generations. The scope of her instruction reached not only the public persona of the princess but also how future royals would fulfil their duties. Today's royals still uphold the deep sense of caring and social responsibility preached by Cartland. Cartland provided a timeless and traditional sense of duty and compassion through her teaching.

Cartland's influence persists, most notably through the royal family's enduring focus on charitable activities and humanitarian work. The Princess of Wales's active participation in charitable works, such as HIV/AIDS awareness, homelessness, and mental health, embodies Cartland's lessons. Advocacy has become a hallmark of the modern royal family, with ever-growing philanthropy, which later generations embrace and expand upon.

Moreover, Cartland's influence on the princess's public image has shaped the media and public relations strategy for subsequent royal family members for decades. Through instruction, she taught that a royal must always maintain poise, dignity, and grace during public scrutiny and take a more active approach to engaging with the press. This is true of the legacy that has been put forward for the current generations of royals on their image, which they now strive to project—having done so under Cartland's guidance.

Aside from the discernible impacts of Cartland's enduring legacy, the personal values and character traits cherished by the royal family were also influenced by her mentorship of the Princess of Wales. As emphasised throughout Cartland's teachings, kindness, empathy, and inclusivity nurtured a culture of compassionate public service leadership within the younger members of the royal family.

As stated above, Cartland's continued guidance moulded the principles and undertakings of the contemporary royal family, strongly impacting their descendants. This goes beyond the person she mentored, stretching to the institution's very core and enduringly influencing the collective attitude towards duty, charity, and grace.

# Wartime Contributions

## SERVICE, SACRIFICE, AND SOCIETY

## The Context of Wartime

The 20th century was characterised by a chaotic period in the world owing to political issues, economic problems, and conflicts between countries. In the context of world powers, there were conflicts like World War I, Continuous Wars between Nations, The collapse of World Empires, and the establishment of Dictatorial Governments. Continuous tensions resulting from these issues worsened and created international relations filled with the context of crisis. It was within this dangerous environment that Barbara, a relatively young writer, was slowly beginning to bloom. The societal alterations, such as the rise of dictatorial governments and the collapse of empires, and worrying problems like economic instability and political unrest, prepared Grant to face a world where peace was continually under threat. As she moved around the upper class, including "the" decision makers, she was able to watch closely the politics and diplomacy that foreshadowed the coming of the world war. Her childhood experience with the diverse factors of fighting, blended with her acute sense of abuse, would enable her to contribute towards the effort of the wartime.

Understanding the intricate web of the conflict-preparing world is important since it gives insight into what factors and beliefs motivated Cartland to transform the narrative of sacrifice and resilience during wars, shaping the narrative during... Understanding this historical context helps illustrate the impact of war on people, society, and countries as it exposes the collective experiences that spanned the globe, crossing borders and cultures during tremendous suffering.

# Barbara Cartland's Early Awareness of Global Conflict

Like many authors, Barbara Cartland lived in a turbulent time when the world suffered from conflict. War is never an easy experience and tends to give people different perspectives. She was fortunate enough to be sheltered from many of the brutality associated with the battle. However, I still believe that taking the brunt of the fight while growing up in the latter half of her life must have affected her personality traits. From her heartstrings to her brain, she must have felt the battle in one way or another. She was always a part of the landscape surrounding the collapse of World War I, consequently being subject to the social and political transformation of the war. This brutally beautiful reality combined the loving yet tragic nature of humanity. Every single event during her life, while I am forming a so-called big picture about Barbara Cartland, shows how much she cares for humanity. The change during the war must have softened her heart, except for the awful amount of destruction and warfare served against humanity during the war period. On a bigger scale, she saw that war had a horrible impact on societies and sympathies, and as society slowly started changing for the better. This softness, combined with the change during world-changing wars and her humble beginnings, must have given her fairly enough confidence during battle-related issues. By the time she was finally ready to experience the harsh nature of the world during her armed confrontation, she reportedly believed that love and compassion were the biggest cures to the sickness of warfare.

Simultaneously, the harsh realities of wartime suffering and deprivation that Cartland personally experienced influenced her to create a legacy of hope and resilience through her literary and philanthropic works. These early experiences were formative in nurturing her sense of responsibility for mitigating the impacts of war on society, thus sowing the seeds for her future contributions towards wartime efforts. Her literature, with its themes of love, hope, and resilience, served as a powerful tool to uplift the spirits of those affected by war, demonstrating the transformative power of storytelling in times of crisis.

# Voluntary Service and Roles in World War II

Cartland vigorously participated in voluntary service and executed several roles during the Second World War that facilitated the support of the war effort. Cartland appreciated the seriousness of the situation and selflessly dedicated herself to serving her country during this difficult period. Understanding the lack of support, she relentlessly gave her time and effort to several charitable causes with great care and responsibility to the people impacted by the war. Through her voluntary efforts, she showed the spirit of zeal and strength that defined the might of the era. These included fundraising campaigns where she aided those suffering due to the war. Her selfless deeds not only greatly assisted the unfortunate but also motivated countless others to offer support for the war efforts. Likewise, she went beyond services defined by conventions, using her creativity to think of fresh ways for her writing skills to benefit the war effort. As a prolific writer, Cartland advocated for the troops by actively engaging in campaigns to raise morale on the home front.

The tireless work she put into helping others through literature assisted in fostering the resilience of the entire nation in such hard times. Further to this, Cartland noted the war's effect on the public and, as a result, performed public speaking engagements designed to drive up support for the war efforts. She helped galvanise aid and a sense of togetherness throughout the nation by articulating the harsh realities of life during the war. For Cartland, serving voluntarily during World War II was one example of many where she selflessly combined her passion for humanitarian causes with her creativity and talents to benefit others. Her achievements tell us of a legacy of devoted service that shall ever endure in its imprint upon history. Her achievements illustrate a profound legacy of devoted service that demonstrates how individual action, no matter the scale, can alter history.

# Humanitarian Efforts and Advocacy for Troops

In the darkness of World War II, Barbara Cartland's spirit and commitment to humanitarian work shone brightly. Aside from her voluntary service and other key responsibilities during the war, she made it a personal mission to advocate for the welfare of the home and battlefront troops. Being deeply aware of soldiers' suffering, Cartland advocated fiercely for their cause to mitigate their suffering and improve their spirits. Grasping the vast impact of literature as a tool of inspiration for servicemen, she desperately wrote letters and dispatches, often adding snippets of romantic tales and uplifting stories to provide respite during the chaos of combat. These literary contributions significantly improved the morale of countless soldiers, allowing them to escape from the grim realities of war through their imagination. Beyond the realm of writing, Cartland employed her powerful contacts to spearhead relief efforts for military personnel to provide them with comforts and necessities. Her relentless advocacy united disparate communities across borders to support and rally for those in uniform.

Her selfless efforts towards mobilising resources and public awareness ensured servicemen's issues remained relevant to societal conversations. Capturing the essence of compassion, she tirelessly strove toward achieving optimal conditions in housing, medicine, and morale, exhibiting deep commitment toward the troops. Cartland transcended the boundaries of conventional warfare and left behind a legacy of compassion which still resonates today. Her enduring humanitarian work and advocacy shaped Cartland's identity as a symbol of hope and unwavering resolve during a period when the need of the hour was renewed responsibility for the brave men and women who dedicated their lives to serving their countries.

# Contributions to Wartime Literature and Propaganda

The British novelist Barbara Cartland undertook the dual challenge of wartime literature and propaganda during WWII. As a public figure already publishing books, she understood the immense impact a single voice could have on public will and propaganda. During this time, Cartland's novels disclosed her unabated sense of responsibility and zealous nationalism. She wanted to encourage civilians and soldiers, and her novels created a fictive buffer where romance, valour, and hope would greet adversity rather than surrender.

As much as she provided an escape through romantic tales, Cartland was also keenly aware of her responsibility to the state and did her share towards the propaganda campaign supporting the war. She rendered concepts of stubbornness, persistence, and togetherness on the pages of her novels, backing the spirit of Brits against forces of evil and subjugation. The underpinning of British defiance and cries of sacrifice was a frequent motif of her fiction, serving as an indirect but effective means of getting support for the war from people sitting in safe homes.

Cartland also worked directly with known propaganda sponsors and the government agencies responsible for these activities, using her skills and fame to support messages proclaiming perseverance and unity.

Her stories were an asset in pro-British circular persuasion and garnering support because her narratives had never-failing audience reception all over the country. British unity and fortitude were a consistent narrative driven through magazines, radio sets, and public appearances, which formed the British psyche during this volatile period of the country.

Aside from written work, Cartland personally participated in various charity drives, demonstrating her unswerving activism for literature in a positive light during calamitous times. Her activism ranged from sponsoring literary sessions, building collections, personally attending to soldiers in hospitals, supporting military and other patients through literary welfare, and raising funds for directly war-affected people. These literary activities, directly and indirectly, served to maintain and bolster international ties, cohesion, and understanding through literature during cultural divergence. Cartland's collective energetic drives worked towards hopeful and brighter feelings for patients hit by war.

Looking at her work in propaganda literature during the British Civil War reveals that Cartland transcended the universe of pure fiction. During the critical historical juncture, she mobilised the forces of popular tales of the realm to reinstate people's image of the British Empire in tune with the state's strategies. Thus, she profoundly influenced the public's perceptions and narratives in history they used and constructed around.

As both an author and a public advocate, Cartland shaped the socio-emotional culture of Britain during the war period through her multifaceted contributions, cementing her legacy as an enduring figure in Britain's history.

## The Social Impact of Wartime Work on Personal Life

In the context of the Second World War, it was almost impossible for Barbara Cartland to maintain her devotion to her wartime responsibilities without somehow impacting her personal life. While she worked on her propaganda projects and later on her literary works of the war period, she was forced to separate her public responsibilities from her personal life. Her work created major social consequences as her public life and self-care routine were no longer separated, giving her public attention in her private space. Additionally, the emotional burden of seeing the consequences of the war on people and societies permanently influenced her relationships and worldview.

Her position as a prominent wartime literature and propaganda figure came with ever-expanding social connections, forcing her into some of the most sought-after diplomatic contacts. The professional friendships and networks with leaders and key figures of her time broadened her scope and perspective on global events and enhanced her social skills. This development added to the already existing complexity of her social standing and managing her expectations regarding responsibilities for her country. Yet, amid the developments of her growing public image, Cartland tried to keep some sense of normalcy in her personal life during the uncertain and turbulent war period. Balancing public attention and personal space became a relentless struggle as Cartland tried to protect her family from the harsh realities of public life while fulfilling her civic duties. Moreover, witnessing the devastation of war and the suffering of those impacted by violence deeply affected Cartland, shaping her behaviour and imprinting her naturally caring personality.

Cartland's public wartime responsibilities immediately impacted her close associates, peripheral social relations, and civic activities. Her new position as an internationally renowned personality brought along many obligations, which, due to their complexity, made it impossible to separate her personal and professional life, further restricting her public and private personas. The changing outlooks and attitudes towards society during the war intensified these issues, forcing Cartland to deal with various social issues in a highly sophisticated manner.

Looking back, the social consequences of Cartland's wartime contributions highlight her character and commitment to her profession. Despite the overwhelming stress in her private life, she pursued a greater purpose, demonstrating remarkable strength and flexibility during the turbulent wartime period.

## Networking Across Borders: Influential Connections

Connecting with people who could make a difference was crucial, especially during conflict and turmoil; in the case of Barbara Cartland, her network extended beyond her country and enabled her to use her influence to further charitable and humanitarian causes. Cartland reached some of the most important people in her country and abroad through her social and diplomatic contacts. With these contacts, she was given an angle of the world different from hers and shaped her philanthropic work to suit the needs of different communities affected by war. Through her philanthropic work, Cartland was able to use her connections with prominent people and organisations not just to supply aid but also to build lasting partnerships across countries. She tried to transform opponents into advocates and those with disparate views into allies. Her example explains how networking goes beyond borders for a social cause.

Even so, Cartland could advocate for post-war recovery policies because she skillfully manoeuvred through the intricate web of political and diplomatic relations. With her powerful contacts, Cartland proved strategic connections could be utilised positively to change the world, heavily influencing the global mindset during the post-war period. The impact of her network is permanently etched into history and inspires modern-day philanthropic initiatives, firmly highlighting the importance of establishing useful connections during crises and rebuilding periods.

# Philanthropy and Support for Post-war Recovery

After the conclusion of the Second World War, Barbara Cartland focused her efforts on philanthropic projects intended for post-war recovery. She was well aware of the destruction the conflict had caused and worked on ways to make the world better for those afflicted by the war. Cartland was deeply concerned about the civilians suffering during the aftermath of the war, especially the children and families who had been most affected by the conflict.

One of her prominent initiatives was setting up numerous charitable foundations to aid war relief regions. With these efforts, she steered some relief towards rebuilding the infrastructure, reviving the medical facilities, and developing education for the poor. Cartland's resolute regard for post-war reconstruction was not limited to the provision of funds alone. She visited the ravaged areas, spoke to the local elders, and lobbied for global volunteers to help deal with the destruction that the war had caused.

Apart from her direct initiatives in philanthropy, Cartland also used her literary eminence to raise funds and create support for post-war relief endeavours. She tried to elevate the plight of the people for public action through written or spoken words and media campaigns to bring hope and life to people in war-affected countries. As an author, she had a strong political influence to resource and create international attention for the people trying to attain normality after the war.

Cartland's aid did not stop at the material level in post-war recovery, as she understood people's emotional and psychological recuperation after the war. She supported efforts that provided counselling, emotional care, and trauma therapy for people who had survived the war, understanding the deep and lasting scars from that period. Cartland's philanthropy was multifaceted, illustrating that she wanted to promote resilience and dignified humanity to people who suffered the miseries of war.

The transformational impact on the communities she assisted vividly illustrates Cartland's philanthropic legacy. She is remembered for the lasting institutions and programmes that embody compassion, solidarity, and construction in war-torn regions. This is the enduring legacy of her post-war contribution; it is a sign of her constant commitment to alleviating people's suffering and building a better world for future generations.

# Reflections on Sacrifice: Personal Insights

Barbara Cartland's wartime experiences shaped her understanding of sacrifice and service. As World War II progressed, she witnessed the enormous destruction that the war inflicted upon people and society as a whole, which made her appreciate the sacrifices both military and civilian personnel made. Cartland's extensive philanthropy work and aid in post-war recovery efforts catalysed her endeavour to address the impacts of sacrifice on society. Her empathy towards people suffering in war-ridden areas demonstrates her compassion that truly knows no bounds.

Cartland had an emotional recollection of people in conflict zones and their suppressed emotions. She praised the astounding courage and resilience of many people who endured unimaginable suffering during the war. These interpretations highlight how strongly Cartland believed in people's resilience within dire and hope-filled situations.

Cartland's sacrifices illustrate the notion of perpetual change through astounding acts of courage and self-endurance. While war raged around her, she recognised the colossal power of will, the human spirit, and the strength of unity in the face of adversity. These thoughts reflected her steadfast devotion to working for the welfare of others, especially those gnawed at by the horrors of war.

Further still, Cartland's reflections explored the paradox of losing something and persevering, making it clear how sacrifice can galvanise individuals and communities with a renewed sense of purpose and resilience. Her narratives evoke profound feelings marked by sacrifice and its enduring influence, inviting society to unite and develop. Through her introspective accounts, she brought forth the overlapping meaning of sacrifice and that humans will always find a way to heal, renew, and unite.

Ultimately, Cartland's reflections on sacrifice remain a powerful testament to the enduring spirit of resilience and selflessness. They demonstrate her enduring commitment to lifting others and cultivating collective strength when facing challenges. Cartland deeply shares her insights so readers are compelled to think about the deep-rooted meaning of sacrifice and its impact on the continuum of humanity and history.

## Legacy of Wartime Contributions in Historical Context

Barbara Cartland's contributions during the war period affected not only the literary world but history as a whole. As the world dealt with the effects and problems set forth by World War II,

Cartland acted as a figure of hope, using her standing to support the war effort. Upon exploring the impact of her wartime contributions during the particular period, one observes that her contributions went beyond the confines of engine romance literature, as she published numerous works to restore hope in her audience.

Her empathic dedication to voluntary service, in conjunction with patriotic fervour spent on boosting the spirits of soldiers and civilians alike, set a standard for social responsibility during that period. Her deeds were not limited to one nation's borders but embraced many cultures and communities, offering sentiments of togetherness. Cartland's humanitarian advocacy and active engagement in post-war recovery initiatives shaped the social structure of a world in need of recovering from a widespread conflict.

In addition to all this, Cartland's Civil Contributions to the war efforts and the literature resulting from them formed a pivotal standpoint on how the populace and the world perceived the war.

Answer the question: "Which events had to take place for Cartland's words to have such a great impact?"

Through vivid imagery, she painted vibrant pictures with her words that distracted an audience from the chaos around them and conveyed valuable information through storytelling that connected people from different places. During these challenging times, her literary work displayed narratives' effectiveness in moulding people's awareness around them and building hope in what is otherwise a bleak reality.

The focus on her personal and work life after the war highlighted the enduring legacy of Cartland's wartime work. The encounters and experiences during this time shaped her later work and advocacy, marking her as an influential person in both the literary and humanitarian world. From the standpoint of hindsight's view of history, Cartland's contributions in the blaring noise of the pre-and post-war world are a reminder of how people can still create meaningful change in any circumstance.

About the reflection on her legacy, the observation presented suggests that Cartland's wartime contributions profoundly echo modern society with ever-present reminders of kindness, tenacity, and the need to stand up in the face of global turmoil.

In our contemporary society, where the remnants of history co-exist with emerging issues, Cartland's wartime achievements remind us of the profound impact one person can have toward forging unity and inciting change, even in the most challenging circumstances.

# Critics vs. Commercial Success

## THE DICHOTOMY OF DEFINITION

## Navigating the Literary Establishment: Initial Reception

Barbara Cartland met with scepticism and curiosity from literary circles as she entered the realm of romantic fiction. Cartland struggled to gain recognition in her attempt to write romantic fiction, which was looked down upon by the literary establishment. The prevailing beliefs about 'serious literature' excluded the romance genre. Cartland faced a formidable challenge in trying to achieve acceptance as an author. Immersed in the highbrow literary world, critics and scholars dismissed her works as lacking artistic value. This disapproval stemmed from a widespread bias against romance fiction. Despite all odds, however, Cartland made a case for important and relevant romantic stories, inherently defying those deeply entrenched biases. Eventually, she paved the way for romance to be considered a vital expression of literature. Through her unyielding dedication and unprecedented output, she embraced the literary establishment's strictures. It is with her undeniable resolve that she challenged the boundaries of literature.

Barbara Cartland's enduring legacy stands as a testament to her ability to withstand initial criticism and affirm the persistent relevance of romance fiction within literature. Her work continues to inspire and influence the romance genre, demonstrating the lasting impact of her contributions.

## Critics' Perspective: Analysing Barbara Cartland's Style

When it comes to Barbara Cartland's literary style, critics have expressed a wide range of views, sparking a lively debate that encapsulates the fundamental arguments surrounding romance fiction as a whole. Some argue that Cartland's prose is overly embellished, with a heavy focus on idealised love and make-believe, while others maintain that her style is an exercise in intent, taking romance writing to new heights through its emotion-laden history and polished diction that captivates. This diversity of opinion adds an intriguing layer to the discussion of literary style.

Critics tend to focus on some of Cartland's recurring motifs and thematic content of her work. The major themes of love, fate, and social barriers are often cited as core elements. Cartland's appeal, using her distinct voice and narrative formula, has captivated generations of readers, and critics examine her enduring allure. Additionally, they consider the complex interplay of character, plot, and history in her writing style and the various meanings it might hold for readers.

The debate surrounding Cartland's style brings into focus the evolving perceptions of literary value and the categorisation of romance as a genre. Critics engage in discussions where popularity and literary value intersect, challenging the notion that commercial success is at odds with artistic merit. Some critics argue against viewing Cartland solely as a commercial writer of lowbrow literature, instead valuing the comfort and cultural importance her work holds as literature. This debate underscores the arbitrariness of literary criticism and the fluidity of standards in defining quality literature.

In the case of Cartland, her style analysis deepens the debate on aesthetic appreciation and public reception of a work. This highlights the intricate dynamic between writers, their books, and the multifaceted readers they attract. Barbara Cartland is the primary focus of this discussion not simply as an author whose work is rich in sociological significance but also as a timeless icon within the popular literary culture and the romance genre whose impact transcended societal boundaries.

## The Commercial Triumph: Unrivaled Popularity and Sales

Barbara Cartland's commercial success, based on her unparalleled popularity and extraordinary sales figures, is a testament to her ability to connect with readers on a profound emotional level. To dismiss her literature would be to overlook how she achieved remarkable sales and remained one of the few authors to produce over 600 titles that captivated the public's attention. Her novels were sought after both in libraries and online booksellers, demonstrating that readers continually sought out great epic and captivating love stories.

Cartland's commercial success is attributed, in no small part, to her ability to connect with her readers on an emotional level. Through her captivating stories and characters, she managed to create portals to worlds suffused with enchanting fantasy. Furthermore, her works' underlying currents of love, honour, and passion enabled countless readers to relate to and appreciate her timeless themes throughout generations.

It is also important to note that Barbara Cartland's novels did not only appeal to traditional print readers. Adapting to changing technologies, her works mastered radio and television by introducing audiobooks and e-books, effectively catering to new audiences with her oeuvre. Her boldness to adapt to new platforms and the ever-changing world reinforced her status as a literary phenomenon whose impact is beyond the world of books.

Moreover, her unique marketing strategies greatly aided Cartland's remarkable sales achievements. She mastered the art of branding, publicity, and self-advertisement, which allowed her to cultivate a captivating public image that bolstered the sales of her books beyond imagination. Through skilful planning, she gave speeches, launched her novels, and interacted with the media in a way that guaranteed sustained excitement and intrigue for each novel before its release.

Although literary critics occasionally criticised her work, Cartland's loyal fans provided unflagging support, confirming the appeal of her romantic tales. One cannot refute that her magical yet idealistic storytelling sharpened her literary phenomenon status and unrivalled success in the world of fiction.

# Literary Critique vs. Reader Delight: A Sym-

# biotic Relationship

The romance fiction industry offers an interplay between literary critique and reader delight. This phenomenon has been of great scholarly interest. Critics define works of romance through the artistic merit of such works, paying attention to whether there is innovation, deep themes, and sophisticated plot construction. In this case, critics of romance literature seek the presence of social individualistic commentary and evaluate the romance's impact on the literary world. For the readers, romantic novels offer hope, joy, and emotional connection that escapes reality, pain, and worries. Escapism continues to be a popular reason for engaging with a book, something many readers seek out. In retreating, they expect to feel better about their realities. The relationship between the critic's delight and the reader's appreciation serves both parties simultaneously.

Romance novels create an important forum for exploring ideas of love, relationships, and self-development, as they are rooted in emotional bonds and relatable themes. The comforting, inspiring, and empowering value of these narratives to countless readers is often ignored, as the critique of repetitive storytelling and predictable resolutions is so common. Emphasis should, however, be placed on the fact that while the romance genre is often dismissed with nothing but scathing critiques, such as the lack of literary depth, a critique always brings an appeal devoid of emotion.

Furthermore, empathy between literary critique and reader pleasure continues to advance the canon of romance literature. The fact that the romance fiction genre does face scrutiny regarding its literary depth indicates its importance. A literary focus which tends to ignore the commercial success of the genre and its lasting cultural significance globally is quite concerning. The powerful ability of the genre to transcend various age demographics also aids in understanding humans, their ideals, and emotions, which is imperative for literature. Recognising the relationship between commercial success and literary merit enables a well-rounded discourse regarding romance fiction's contributions to literature and readers' lives.

Critical analysis paired with joy as a reader contributes to the wholesome appreciation of romance fiction. Appreciating the interplay of literary critique and reader delight allows for a more nuanced and holistic view of the genre's cultural significance, emotional resonance, and legacy.

## Evolving Definitions of Quality: The Role of Romance Fiction

In literary circles, their constituents have faced the test of time and endured evolution. This flux is perhaps most noticeable in the case of romance fiction, where the clash between critical appraisal and devoted readerships has led to a rethinking of literary value. Traditionally, literary value rested primarily on the intricacy, profundity, and originality within a given work; these measures are now being widened to include the emotional appeal, escapism, and empowerment that define romance narratives. The unabated appeal of romance fiction and the works of Barbara Cartland demand a reassessment of how we regard and value this branch of literature. An important part of this shift is acknowledging the ability of romance fiction to address certain fundamental human processes that provide comfort, hope, and cleansing relief to many readers, regardless of their background. Also, the treatment of such subjects as love, enduring struggle, and self-renewal in the setting of romance fiction illustrates its ability to reflect and shape the human experience in complex realities. Now, with the ever-growing focus on inclusivity and diversity within the genre, the concept of romance fiction has become a window for muted communities and marginalised voices, fostering empathy, understanding, and social consciousness.

This evolution also includes conversations about the politics of the democratisation of literature, which challenges elitist taste (as a clear indicator of power relations) in favour of the democratic value of "reader satisfaction". Inevitably, the revisions in romance fiction also signal cultural shifts in the literary landscape's spelling and politics of inclusivity. The evolving standards of assessing literary merits have accentuated and positioned romance fiction as a genre that dominates the traditional hierarchy of artistic value.

The romance fiction scenario illustrates the relentless valuation of literary standards, exemplifying the indelible movements within the literary canon and the quest for understanding narrative artistry more deeply. These shifts make it apparent that romance fiction permeates beyond the realm of abnormal entertainment; it sheds light on social realities, functions as social discourse, and epitomises the enduring significance of storytelling.

## Cartland's Response to Criticism: Defending a Genre

Barbara Cartland, as the prolific author of romantic fiction, consistently faced criticism and skepticism from literary circles. Cartland staunchly defended her chosen genre, often expressing her unwavering commitment to the romance novel. In response to detractors who dismissed romance fiction as formulaic or lacking in literary merit, Cartland emphasized the profound emotional impact and escapism that her novels provided to readers. She firmly believed that the art of storytelling should prioritize uplifting and comforting the audience, which she accomplished through her exquisite narratives of love, passion, and triumph over adversity.

Cartland vehemently rejected the notion that romance novels were simplistic or superficial. Instead, she viewed them as an essential form of entertainment and solace, especially during challenging times. Drawing on her own experiences and observations, Cartland eloquently articulated how romance fiction served as a beacon of hope for countless individuals, offering reassurance and fostering a belief in the power of love. Moreover, she underscored the significance of nurturing imagination and optimism through her stories, dismissing criticisms that failed to acknowledge the profound cultural impact of romance literature.

In her defense of the romance genre, Cartland emphasized that her works transcended typical conventions, incorporating historical accuracy, social commentary, and intricate character development. She highlighted the extensive research and attention to detail that underpinned her novels, challenging critics to recognize the complexity and depth within her storytelling. Cartland's response to criticism extended beyond a personal defense; it encompassed a broader advocacy for celebrating diverse literary expressions and respecting the varied tastes of readers worldwide.

Furthermore, Cartland addressed the gendered biases that often colored perceptions of romance fiction, asserting that the genre's dismissal reflected entrenched prejudices against topics traditionally associated with women's interests. She challenged the pervasive stereotypes, arguing that romance literature deserved recognition as a legitimate and valued form of artistic expression. By advocating for inclusivity and embracing the emotional resonance of romance, Cartland sought to elevate the genre's status and dismantle the barriers that marginalized its contributions to the literary landscape.

Ultimately, Cartland's response to criticism encapsulated a steadfast dedication to championing the enduring appeal and significance of romance fiction. Her resolute defense not only validated the genre's relevance but also advanced a spirited dialogue on the evolving dynamics of literature and cultural discourse. Through her impassioned advocacy, Cartland left an indelible mark on the literary world, shaping the ongoing narrative of romance fiction's artistic merits and enduring impact.

## Cultural Impact: Beyond Commercial Metrics

The literary works of Barbara Cartland have profoundly influenced the world's culture, leaving an indelible mark that extends beyond mere commercial success. Her romance stories have affected the thoughts and lives of people on a far deeper level than what is considered conventional success. The extensive readership associated with her love stories symbolises their importance as cultural phenomena, transcending even more audiences of all ages, races, and nationalities over different years and across the world.

From evaluating the impact at the level of society, it is clear that Cartland's contribution as a mere entertainer is insufficient. For now, she has secured a place in society's cherished expressions of love, hope, and nostalgia. More than a prolific author, an influencer of emotions and dreams, Cartland advances into the core of people's thoughts, redeeming themes where she romances and celebrates enduring honour and steadfast tenacity. Through the portrayal of idealised love together with virtuous characters, powerful mirrors drawing upon society's longing and values are raised, further fostering perceptions around the notions of chivalry, romance, and feminine agency. As such, works of this nature have come to epitomise enduring culture and virtue.

The adaptations of Cartland's works to films, television, and even stage productions have further built her presence in popular culture. Such adaptations have undoubtedly fortified the understanding of her stories and narratives while strengthening their influence on audience perception and interpretation. Moreover, her narratives are still relevant in contemporary adaptations, which speaks to the resonance of her cultural significance and impact as a writer. Also, her ideals captured through media have visually contributed greatly towards the everlasting imprint she has on society. This is how Cartland's legacy is preserved, promoting an ethos that continuously fortifies society and time. Thus, the impact of Cartland's literature is not solely bounded within the domain of literary literature; she is respected and cherished as a cultural guide and defender of romantic traditions.

# Media Influence: Shaping Public Perception

The media's influence on public perception, especially in the case of Barbara Cartland's public career, is important to consider. Throughout her career, Cartland was advertised almost everywhere in the media, which speaks greatly of her success as a writer, and her image was carefully crafted to capture the attention of people of all ages. Also, through various interviews, photoshoots, and public appearances, she attempted to act as the epitome of romance and grace, helping her brand herself as an alluring beauty of a writer. More importantly, the media sought plenty of publicity opportunities to expand public perception surrounding Cartland and the entire realm of romance novels. Using numerous newspapers, magazines, and even television shows to express their admiration of her work, the media helped cement Cartland's stature as an author, commanding public admiration and, thus, curiosity about her persona. That carefully cultivated mystique increased book purchases and entrenched public perception of her as a standard of romantic fantasy.

The media's attitude toward the works of Cartland dominated the polemic opinion surrounding romance fiction, too. By advertising Cartland's achievements in literature and branding her as an icon, the media depicted romance as something people should aspire to—mingled with stagnant adoration—and a sophisticated escape. This role of the media in shaping public perception is significant and has contributed to the widespread acceptance of romance literature.

Therefore, this particular representation contributed to the public's understanding of Cartland's work and the entirety of the romance genre. It shifted its perception from being regarded merely as entertainment to a prized aspect of literature. Alongside these developments, however, the media's impact did spark controversy regarding the validity of romance fiction. Critics claimed that the media's coverage of Cartland's novels exaggerated their importance, stripping them of their artistic value and leading people to misjudge the genre's sophistication. Supporters, conversely, claimed that the media's focus on Cartland's work widened audience appreciation for the theme of love in literature; therefore, the portrayal of romance novels was an important step towards accepting them in popular culture. Media attention influenced how the public viewed Barbara Cartland, the media character, and her literary works, thus shaping her legacy and the perception of romance fiction within literature.

# The Balance of Art and Commerce: Defining Literary Success

Even today, the duality of art and commerce in literature remains relevant. This divide is particularly notable in romance fiction, where the sales milestones of authors such as Barbara Cartland clash with the pronounced critiques of her literary talent. Understanding the many dynamics of popular fiction adds layers to considering literary success.

Literary success is a multifaceted term that can mean different things, such as the artistic nature of the writing or the appeal it garners from readers. About authors like Cartland, the dilemma stems from her tremendous sales figures and constant critical bashing. The context shifts in the backdrop of a genre that has long been disdained and looked down upon by the literary elite when viewed from the angle of value placed within the evaluation of success.

The popularity of Cartland's work demonstrates how her storytelling engages with millions of people, earning her fans across the globe. Still, her success raised eyebrows concerning the literary depth and quality of her work due to its commercial nature. Nevertheless, one cannot ignore the depths of many works that offer many readers soothing escapism and emotional fulfilment. It is essential to recognise the influence and importance of captivating narratives.

Her ability to define success in literature can be considered strange as romance fiction. Cartland's works require the reader to understand the purpose of fulfilling the multifaceted needs and wants of the audience, which is equally diverse. Cartland's works might not fit into the so-called classic standards of literature. Still, her ability to capture universal themes under the banner of love, hope, and resilience showcases the significance of romantic stories in humanity's ever-evolving tale.

Additionally, the coming together of the fields of art and business in literature evokes consideration of the changing nature of the industry and the telling of stories by different people. The telling of stories by different people provides an opportunity for more representation, which moves the success of literature to a whole new level. In this case, authors like Cartland exemplify how commercial success is achieved due to popular fiction embracing culture and shaping people's ideas and opinions.

As stated previously, the definition of success in literature should include consideration of success in the broader, multiple genres and definitional layers of literature and its readership. Therefore, the consideration of the balance between art and commerce is less restricted to the boundaries of achievement when looking at success but rather viewed from the angle of the power embedded in literature to unite, motivate, and outlive its readers.

# Enduring Popularity: The Undeniable Ap-

# peal

Following Barbara Cartland's success, she remains one of the most popular authors in fiction due to her undeniable appeal, which directly marks her enduring popularity. It is important to highlight that while facing strong opposition from the conservative literary world, Cartland has been winning the affection of countless readers.

Cartland is still popular today because of her ability to understand human emotions and her skills in portraying romances that appeal to most people. Her love stories contain themes of love, honour, and virtue, which transcend generations and offer an escape into a world of elegance and wonder where happy endings are guaranteed.

Her vivid descriptions of extravagant settings, balls filled with dashing heroes, and captivating heroines transport readers to another time. Cartland's intricate attention to detail, mixed with captivating prose, provides an element of escapism, which has aided in her sustaining appeal.

Furthermore, Cartland's reputation is buoyed by her 700 novels over nearly seventy years. In addition to her epic output, Cartland's influence is everlasting due to her unwavering commitment to delivering captivating romance fiction.

Her writing contains elegant prose interspersed with uplifting and cheerful undertones, ensuring readers of all ages become engrossed. This approach has allowed her to establish an internationally devoted fanbase, ensuring the legacy of her beautiful tales will never fade.

Besides the social level of Cartland's works, her influence is felt in other areas as well. Through her active participation in fashion and social charity work, she has won the admiration of many and maintained her public image. This has made her even more popular among the public.

No matter how hard the world of literature changes, new tastes in entertainment keep emerging, and Cartland's books strike the right chord with both new and old readers alike. The hope, joy, and romance that fill her stories guarantee that Cartland's legacy will continue to be cherished for decades and earn her a permanent spot in the history of romance literature.

# Legacy of Love

## CARTLAND'S CONTINUED RELEVANCE

## Enduring Influence on Modern Romance

Even while Barbara Cartland is not classically known today, her work has undoubtedly served as a foundational pillar for modern romantic literature, as it continues to inspire many authors chronologically after her works. She - A Woman's World is one of the most "chronologically" cited works in her love saga novels. She underwent a shift in life when society lost her money at once, returning from there to be at the centre of envy for millions of women who learned through her novel that love can be possible for anyone; it doesn't depend well on time. Her ways of writing books have helped develop women's fiction worldwide, and her style of linking current events to a novel that would encapsulate the era was nothing short of brilliant.

Every one of her noble works had one idea attached to it. That idea was borrowed from Arnold Bennett - Cartland wanted to depict novels that were not considered suitable for common people but were, in fact, perfect for middle-class people. No matter the fate or provocations, love triumphs over all, and that remains the defined central theme for both of her works in every booking saga she undertook, which were connected to and primarily set around the most influential people of that era, showcasing every one of their struggles. For Bearula Speller, the romance novels she read were fresh nor enveloped with a focus on one attachment. What Cartland loved to anchor the table that warmth of queen of the corner was broken over what? This is about the pride of a writer who ended her life facing various controversies over her novel instead of peace, for the main reason was the queen received unexpected freedom in the modern world of grace-loving.

Her romantic novels are undergirded by remarkable attention to historical facts, which has inspired other writers to blend love stories with a rich sense of era and geography brimming with memories. The historical worlds she created for her characters were associated with deep emotions and the standard of romance growing up in today's world had to strive hard to achieve. Today's romance writers must remember the entire package of the touching book and romance in every season for lovers.

Furthermore, the timeless charm of Cartland's writings is reflected in the modern revival of historical romances, which now honour her style with infusions. She continues to be reworked by writers who imbue their tales with swashbuckling lead males and valiant women, with exaggerated tales of love and courtship paying homage to the time-tested romance traditions. Through this engagement with Cartland's works, contemporary romance authors pay tribute to her enduring influence on the genre, ensuring that the echo of her indelible imprint on the world of literature withstands the passage of time for writers and readers.

## Adaptations and Media Presence

Barbara Cartland's contributions have not only transformed the romantic fiction genre but have also transcended to have an impact in various media forms. Cartland's stories have been transformed into films and television shows and published through digital sources, preserving her legacy as a cornerstone in popular culture. Numerous award-winning novels published by Barbara Cartland have received television series adaptations and even movies, maintaining the enchanting nature of her narratives while extending the reach of her appeal. More importantly, the intricate emotions, romanticised historical settings, and sophisticated love stories for which Cartland is known have been fully captured in these adaptations.

The everlasting attraction of Cartland's themes has been captured by modern-day media, where her stories are retold to younger audiences in contemporary adaptations. Barbara Cartland's remarkable ability to tell stories that captivate people of different ages and cultures shows how deeply rooted her work is in media today.

The blend of literature alongside the visual arts has greatly helped maintain Cartland's contributions to the romance genre, which marks her as a literary figure whose influence lives on even today.

# Barbara Cartland's Contribution to Romantic Tropes

The central aspect of Cartland's contribution to romantic tropes is the depiction of true love. In her prolific work, she dominantly showcased the strength of unwavering and pure love throughout history. Her heroines were always graceful and regal, while her heroes featured range and colossal devotion. These strong/courageous champions have set the bar for romance, archetypal fiction 'Cherished' and 'Wield,' lovers, and purveyors of sentiment.

Cartland has had a unique and profound impact on the vast world of romance literature by focusing on a love-conquering-all approach. Her fans were constantly encouraged through her works as true love's ever-present victory over numerous obstacles deeply inspired hope within her readers. This trademark became synonymous with her resonating narrative style and became a vivid reality for her readers and herself.

She did not only concentrate on love; she mastered the ability to focus on romantic life as a means of escape to a fantasy world. The evergreen ballrooms, splendid country houses, and chivalric exploits served as the entrance to her world of imagination. By centring extravagant details and employing graceful adjectives, many devoted lovers and admirers worldwide were bewitched into a fascinating world where love and beauty always existed.

Additionally, by linking herself to the Regency period, a historical period in the early 19th century known for its elegance and social change, Cartland singlehandedly revived the endless arranged marriages, romantic drama, and speculative society. At the same time, she altered the readers' perceptions of historical novels and specially crafted a landscape for countless sub-genres in the broad domain of romantic fiction.

In addition to the narrative aspects of her oeuvre, Cartland also influenced romantic tropes by representing enduring values such as honour, integrity, and virtue. These characters served as paragons of hope for readers who sought virtue and moral strength amid the turmoil of romantic entanglements.

Barbara Cartland will always be revered for her exceptional contribution to the romantic genre, having singlehandedly produced an unmatched legacy of timeless themes and evocative imagery. Her contributions were boundless from the beginning, for she wrote with purity, fervour, and a strong measure of sentiment. She has inspired generations of romance novelists with these qualities and will forever remain the most influential figure in the genre's signature tropes.

## Scholarly Analysis and Literary Recognition

The oeuvre of Barbara Cartland is one of the most explored works among academics and critics specialising in romance literature. They examine the socio-historical context and the stylistic devices underlying the themes presented in her novels, which are considered numerous. Such studies debate how Cartland novelised the notions of gender expectations and historical contexts and idealised love and relationships.

The recognition of Cartland's works goes beyond the long-existing intellectual discourse. As a writer with more than 700 novels, she is regarded as one of history's most prolific popular writers. The fact that she is included in literary canons and her books continue to be loved by many makes her a controversial figure of recognition. Through different analytical lenses, her stylised and multigenerational appeal monologues, dialogues, and plots bind her as one of the most important authors of romantic fantasies.

As noted, one of the most important acknowledgements signifying her recognition as an author is the honours and prestigious awards bestowed upon her. The magnitude of her works and their status as bestsellers earned her recognition from numerous literary and non-literary bodies. By introducing the Special Award of the International Society for Educational Information and Outstanding Achievement Award of the Romantic Novelists Trust, those who acknowledge and appreciate Cartland's recognition emphasise that it is not just due to commercialised notoriety but remains rooted in lasting significance as an author.

Along with receiving praise from critics, her inclusion in curricula and seminar classes indicates that she is respected for her work in the genre. Work on her texts has appeared in different academic settings, and students and researchers can perform thorough studies on her style and imaged subjects. This enduring interest from Cartland's academic circles illustrates that her works still have importance and value as a subject for academic attention.

Such intellectual attention focuses on the study and recognition of Barbara Cartland's works, confirming not only her significance in the development of the romance genre but also highlighting the scope of her impact in the context of literature as a whole.

## Cultural Impact Across Generations

Barbara Cartland's writing has been a source of inspiration for various people, popularising her works. Her work goes beyond the boundaries of romance literature because it reaches the sphere of media, entertainment, and even public life. Elements such as love, gallantry, and grace, Cartland's romantic stories' foundation, have deeply anchored society's perception of romance and courtship for decades.

Cartland's ideals and motifs about romantic love have influenced various cultural products such as movies, television shows, and even fashion. Her enduring aesthetic has undergone innumerable adaptations and narratives, perpetuating her spectacular perception of love within modern frameworks. Moreover, Cartland's impact can also be noted in the sustained popularity of romantic escapist fantasies that enchant audiences and offer relief in today's complicated world.

Cartland's cultural influence can be understood in developing a highly desirable romantic image outside entertainment. Her notions about elegance, moral rectitude, and true love shaped societal standards of romance and encouraged people towards acts of chivalry and genuine emotion. The fact that her literature has remained relevant for so long reveals the extent of Cartland's impact on society's perception of romance, showing how her literary teachings transcend multiple mediums of romance and blend different cultures.

Through the intergenerational sharing of Cartland's romantic philosophy, a sense of uniformity and lineage has been nurtured in the depiction of love and courtship. Cartland's cultural legacy acts as a conduit for older conventions of romance to be reimagined and bloom for modern times, infusing contemporary society with enduring admiration for romantic customs across generations.

Through their rich symbolism and emotion, Cartland's narratives have imprinted enchantment and romance on popular culture. Her impact is a testament to the undying appeal of love stories and the timelessness of Cartland's romance framework.

# Philanthropy and Social Advocacy

Barbara Cartland's literary masterpiece is globally renowned, but her life's work extended beyond writing. Her philanthropy and social advocacy, which were remarkably exceptional, significantly influenced her literary legacy. She dedicated herself to philanthropic activities, advocating for the welfare of the poor and other marginalised groups. Her unwavering support for social charities and other agencies demonstrated her intent to use her influence for good.

One of Cartland's most remembered charitable acts was her participation in fundraising and other humanitarian activities during times of war and crises. She participated in fundraising campaigns and other relief operations, using the general public's image and her social connections to get help for people who were truly suffering. Her compassionate heart and instinct led her to try to reduce violence and spread goodwill to the world.

Alongside her humanitarian work, Cartland was a social activist who addressed healthcare, education, and women's rights issues. Her unreserved advocacy amplified suppressed voices and served as a motivating force for social overhaul. Utilising her stature as a well-known author and public personality, she discussed important socio-cultural matters, which initiated constructive dialogues and prompted decisive actions in people's lives.

Additionally, Cartland focused on women's empowerment and gender egalitarianism through her advocacy work. Her successful attempts to change societal perceptions of women and encourage them to actively pursue their goals testified to her pioneering spirit and unyielding commitment to social justice. She articulated the possibility of carving out identity options beyond traditional gender restrictions. She called upon them to pursue their ambitions, profoundly altering the history of gender relations through her writings and public activities.

The legacies of Barbara Cartland's philanthropy and social advocacy bear witness to her enduring foundation and the values of reverence and advocacy propagated globally toward her. Her commitment to compassion exemplifies the undying essence of her spirit for humanity, philanthropy, and social welfare.

# Preservation of Personal Archives

Barbara Cartland's personal archives, meticulously preserved, serve as a treasure trove for researchers, biographers, and fans of her literary works. These archives, which include her letters, diaries, manuscripts, and personal artefacts, provide a unique insight into her creative process, life, and the historical events that shaped her novels.

This collection includes a wide variety of materials, such as all the covers of her novels and even letters to renowned figures in literature, politics, and entertainment circles. These documents offer insight into not only her thinking and reasoning but also the hurdles she encountered while attempting to publish her novels, as they exhibit themes cherished by people for decades.

Moreover, the upkeep of Cartland's archives has allowed for a deep insight into her social, philanthropic, and advocacy activities. Details pertaining to her philanthropy, public engagements, and partnership activities with diverse groups are interspersed within these files. The meticulous compilation of such documents has revealed her life beyond that of a romance fiction writer.

The collection comprises written documents as well as artefacts belonging to Cartland, such as her dresses, jewellery, and other personal items. These artefacts document her grace and fashion and link to the past periods she beautifully portrayed in her books. By maintaining these artefacts, posterity will have the opportunity to experience the social and aesthetic backdrop forming Cartland's public life framework.

It should be highlighted that the digitisation of the archives has expanded the research and access opportunities for interested scholars worldwide. People can now access Cartland's world through online repositories, digital exhibitions, and the Internet, which enhances the freedom to access her works without limitations of distance or time.

The meticulous preservation of Barbara Cartland's personal archives elucidates her enduring prominence in the literary world. Such collections commemorate her life and inspire, educate, and entertain people through romance, literature, and captivating stories.

## Continuing Fanbase and Global Reach

Barbara Cartland's literary works are yet to fade into obscurity, as a cult following for her novels spans across nations and cultures. Even today, people from all over the globe indulge in the heroic tales and timeless romances infused in her books. This widespread appeal is due to the unyielding love, hope, and honour captured in her prose, which transcends every societal boundary.

Cartland's influence is not limited to the English-speaking world, for her books translated into multiple languages enable her legacy to proliferate in international markets. People from different cultures have appreciated her stories, which have been beloved and transformed into other media like television shows and films, boosting their popularity even more. This wide expansion of her fanbase demonstrates the enduring impact of Cartland's storytelling alongside the perennial appeal of classic romance.

Also, new digital means of interaction with Cartland's works allow modern readers to discover her writings and join the community of readers who appreciate her literary works. Online sites, e-books, and audiobooks offer easier access to Cartland's great cache of romantic fiction and open up new horizons for the contemporary audience while ensuring her legacy lives on for future generations.

The worldwide popularity of Barbara Cartland's novels is a testament to the enduring impact of her storytelling. Despite changing fads and societal shifts, readers around the world continue to find comfort and inspiration in Cartland's narratives of ardent love and devotion. This enduring global appeal is a powerful reminder of the timeless influence of her stories and the deep bond she forges with her readers.

The creation of fandoms, both online and offline, is a testament to the profound impact of Cartland's novels on the lives of her readers. These communities not only celebrate her works, but also provide a platform for fans to share their stories and impressions inspired by her novels. These interactions foster a sense of camaraderie among fans and contribute to the evolution of Cartland's literary world, ensuring it transcends generations.

At her core, Barbara Cartland's global impact and fanbase are solidifying her legacy as a bestselling author whose works evoke deep emotional connections while demonstrating affection throughout the world. The novels beget a legacy of romance throughout pages, borders, and language and remind every reader, young or old, of the enduring charm of love, passion, and optimism embedded in each narrative.

## Overall Sales and Market Legacy

Barbara Cartland's celebrated career as a romance author places her in history as the bestselling writer in that category. Emerging from her sustained appeal is the astounding figure of sales, in contradiction to her popularity, which corroborates her standing as the greatest seller in the history of publishing. She has written more than seven hundred novels and, in turn, gained a stiff total sales number and became a major writer in the realm of romance.

Her books are translated into almost every language, allowing people from different cultures and societies to access them. This aids in broadening the reach of her market legacy and establishes her as a renowned name in literature across the world.

The continued demand for Cartland's novels also reinforces her perennial literary significance. Her works persist in charming many, even in the age of technological advancement, due to the irresistible fascination with historical romance. Her evergreen storytelling imbued with romance, adventure, and virtue has earned her consistent commercial success.

Moreover, Cartland's market imprint also includes audiobooks and print and non-print versions of her work. She has embraced modern technology, and her works have adapted to Aureate, e-books, and audio, ensuring continual relevance and unprecedented accessibility in the modern world. Through e-books and audio adaptations, Cartland's narratives mesmerise today's readers, underscoring her profound market presence.

Apart from direct sales of books, she is also credited with merchandise, films, and other spin-offs which exemplify her market imprint. Her brand's vibrant merchandising, including apparel, ornaments, and memorabilia, showcases the enduring affection for her characters and stories. Moreover, adaptations from novels to films have exposed her works to an even broader audience, enhancing her market and visual media presence.

As a whole, Barbara Cartland's market legacy is characterised by enduring resonance and profitability. Her enduring stories continue to captivate readers worldwide, regardless of time or place. Cartland's unyielding market impact remains a vital component of her literary legacy through the extensive reach of her novels, film adaptations, and even merchandise.

## Tributes and Memorials

Virtually every literature and romance aficionado recognises Cartland's influence. As a result, a plethora of tributes and memorials have been established in her honour. Her recognition continues to grow as new and old fans celebrate her contributions through various commemorative activities. Numerous markers and plaques were erected in her birthplace of Hatfield, England, that relate to significant aspects of her life, allowing tourists to appreciate the sites that sparked her imagination and her childhood, which shaped her literary career.

Literary festivals and events held in her honour illustrate her deep appreciation for her work. Students, scholars, and even aspiring writers attend such events, fostering a sense of admiration for her impact. On a different note, several academic institutions have created grants and scholarships focusing on the study of romantic fiction as a means to honour Cartland's legacy. These actions celebrate her as a literary figure and motivate new storytellers to find joy in their craft. In further honouring her, libraries and museums have begun to host showcases containing her personal belongings, manuscripts, and original artworks, offering a glimpse into her life and culture. In this regard, she has also become a source of inspiration for numerous charitable causes and organisations she once supported, allowing them to enjoy sustained attention and funding in her honour.

Her philanthropic efforts related to helping animals, humanitarian work, and literacy programmes bear witness to her kind nature and commitment to making the world a better place.

Internationally recognised literary awards honoured Cartland for her unique influence by establishing sections bearing her name or stipulations embodying her genre-shaping contributions. These prestigious awards epitomising her remembrance reinforce her enduring legacy while inspiring modern authors to aspire to her artistic ideals. Most notably, modern digital and social media serve as new ways to honour Cartland's influence by enabling people worldwide to participate in virtual discussions, fan clubs, and online activities aimed at keeping her memory alive. With the help of hashtags, virtual archives, and participatory initiatives, her admirers advocate for preserving her enduring impact on romance literature as a testament to literary culture.

# Conclusion

## DEFINING A GENRE FOR GENERATIONS

### Reflecting on an Illustrious Career

With more than 700 published novels to her name, it is no surprise Barbara Cartland is known as one of the most prominent and powerful authors of romance literature. She is revered as an unparalleled figure in the literary world, and her prolific career until her passing at age 98 is a testament to this fact. With stories full of charm and intricate detail, each crafted to instil a sense of romance, she continues to capture the hearts of readers across the globe, demonstrating the universality and inclusivity of her work. From her first novel, published at 21, to the rest of her immense works, it is apparent Cartland holds a unique place in the world of literature.

Not only is Cartland a pioneer for the historical romance genre – maintaining meticulously detailed research steeped in exuberant storytelling – she is also beloved for portraying powerful females who take centre stage. With so many important figures re-entering the literary world and generating interest among the youth like never before, her work is being praised and gaining a newfound following.

Milestones celebrate Cartland's life as she continues to progress as a writer and cultural figure. Her recognition as the Queen of Romance and the awarding of Dame Commander of the Order of the British Empire (DBE) for her charity services in literature strengthen her legacy. Most famously, her unmatched success led to a spot in the Guinness World Records book for being the most prolific author, alongside other literary elites.

Also, Cartland's impact is far more far-reaching than the walls of traditional literature. Her advocacy of romantic ideals and her efforts towards many philanthropic causes show her strong character in trying to spread love and compassion. She used her platform to support many causes that were close to her heart and, as a result, changed the literary world and society.

To sum up, Barbara Cartland's impressive career is a Roll of Honour signifying literary greatness. She is a leader in romance literature thanks to her never-ending passion towards writing fairy tales and preserving the values of love and chivalry. Her legacy, which will continue to inspire hundreds of readers and writers with her exceptional imagination and devotion, ensures a sense of continuity and connection to the past.

# The Hallmarks of a Cartland Romance

As an author, Cartland was adept at capturing romance to the extent that it became the identity of the person. She carved out her own unique niche in the genre of romantic literature, infusing her works with a distinct charm and elegance. Every novel that she wrote bore the hallmarks that define a Cartland romance, and with this, she transformed storytelling into something more beautiful than just words.

All Cartland romances share traits, one of which is love in its purest form. Suffering through various forms of conflict, Cartland's protagonists endure so much yet somehow hold onto the beacon of love's promise. Escorting readers alongside, Cartland serves them immense hope and inspiration by portraying love so unwaveringly. This love resonates deeply with audiences and paints the picture of her understanding of a heart so complex.

Portraying history's elegance and opulence goes hand in hand with Cartland's romantic narratives. Chandeliers, ballrooms, and period attires innumerable make their place in her novels, serving as a backdrop that enhances the romantic elements of her stories. Cartland describes them in such detail that her audience becomes transposed into a period where charm and sophistication are paramount. The facts woven into her stories serve to further heighten the narrative while captivating readers into a world that is rich in beauty.

Cartland has also blended chivalry and honour into her stories, showcasing good virtues and gallantry. Her heroes display courage, fidelity, and selfless devotion, considering a softened version of manhood that is still popular. These attributes enhance the romantic relationships among the characters within Cartland's stories and convey important values about honour and goodness.

Winning over challenges is one theme present in all of Cartland's books. These themes give positive energy and a fresh perspective to her storytelling. Her protagonists struggle with difficult obstacles that include social and personal challenges, such as societal expectations and personal sacrifices. They eventually win these battles alongside love and happiness. Readers are likely to feel the effect of this combination of underlying themes along with inspirational strength.

The trademarks of a Cartland romance invite readers into a world where love is all-powerful, and courage blends seamlessly with decency, transcending time and culture. These themes of romance and dedication are captured in her works, making them a treasured part of literary heritage and guaranteeing that Cartland will remain a beacon of romantic writing for centuries to come.

## Evolving Perceptions: A Historical Context

The analysis of romance literature has been regarded with varying levels of interest throughout history. This directly reflects the values, standards, and ideologies of every socio-historical period and is intricately woven with people's history. Considering the history of Barbara Cartland's life and works, it is evident that her writings actively shaped and accepted sentiments of romance literature. Shifting focus towards the early 20th century, which is considered the period of intense social change and the advent of new lifestyles (including new forms of gendered social roles), it is observable that Cartland's narratives attempted to alleviate the hopelessness and depression caused by wars. Her stories transported readers to realms of glamour, chivalry and unconditional love, outlooks that were a way to rise above in trying times. In the middle of the 20th century, when society, struggling with the zest of cultural movements and the much-awaited woman's liberation, began to shift toward accepting Cartland's powerful feminine protagonists and tales of undying love, Cartland began to gain popularity, enabling women through fiction celebrating their fantasies. This set her increasingly at odds with the prevailing sentiments and further cemented her status as a leading force in the evolution of romantic literature.

In the 20th century, the emergence of new literary theories, especially post-modernism, reevaluating traditional genres was a critical turning point in the propagation of classic romanticism. During this wave of critical scrutiny, Cartland was still writing her works, which gave her readers enduring insights into timeless values through adaptation to modern sensibilities. Studying Cartland's novels deeply reveals the historical context and regions of constant patterns in literature intertwined with the socio-cultures of each period. Additionally, this study can help understand Cartland's work's cross-temporal impact on the romantic literature genre and appeal beyond the timeframe to the landscape of ever-shifting romantic literature.

# Influence on Contemporary Romantic Literature

The influence of Barbara Cartland's romantic novels is unquestionable and ever-lasting in contemporary romantic literature. Her stunning stories of huge romances featuring historical contexts with extraordinary central characters have remarkably cemented the genre. The way Cartland tells her love stories filled with adventure and gallantry has profoundly influenced how modern authors approach romantic fiction.

One of Cartland's trademarks was heroines who empowered

themselves, which affects modern romantic literature today and is perhaps why Cartland is so influential. Through her characters, she showed the strength of femininity and the woman's ability to control her life and fate even in difficult circumstances. Without a doubt, this theme has been passed down through many generations and even in contemporary literature, women are still writing about self-sufficient protagonists who are strong and resilient.

Meticulous attention to historical details, as Cartland showed, also affects romantic fiction, particularly in the development of its authenticity. Describing the bygone days along with society's manners and customs and portraying vivid images is a requisite that modern authors have to meet if they want to capture the imagination of their readers. Her painstaking and precise research has enriched descriptive works of romantic literature because readers are invited to travel through time and experience various cultures.

Moreover, the study of Cartland's enduring romantic themes, such as second-chance love, first encounters, and love transforming individuals, influenced contemporary writers to rework these themes. These motifs are enduring and appealing in Cartland's works. They continue to captivate readers and serve as a fountain of inspiration for modern writers looking to evoke emotional responses.

In addition to thematic influence, her elegant prose and enchanting narrative style have tremendously changed romance storytelling's craft. Cartland's ability to capture love and passion with lyricism and poetic imagery influenced aspiring authors who wished to portray romance's enchanting beauty. Writers aim for emotions that appeal to the senses, which is heavily relied on, guiding authors to sculpt clever, expressive prose that touches on a deeper level.

In closing, Barbara Cartland's impact on modern romantic literature showcases her influence. The world has been and continues to be grateful for her work. From enchanting her readers with epic tales of love, adventure, and undying loyalty to romantic fiction, her captivating plots remain unparalleled.

## Cultural Imprint and Global Reach

The inescapable influence of Cartland's books is evident in contemporary popular culture worldwide, without restrictions on age, language, or culture. The audience from different regions of the world certainly connects with her books because of the themes of love, honour, and indomitable spirit. It is fascinating that people worldwide still enjoy reading Cartland's books due to the timeless portrayal of historical settings and societal dynamics.

Cartland's translations into several languages enabled the broad spread of romance and storytelling, making her a well-known author across the globe. Her stories have shaped romance novels and even the greater cultural world. This is visible in fashion, arts, entertainment, and many other areas. Through adaptations, references, and even parody, Cartland has influenced how we perceive love and shaped the cultural imagination.

Equally important, the ethos contained within Cartland's works has greatly contributed to the understanding and appreciation of different cultures. By appealing to the humanistic aspects of her narrative, people from different cultures came together to appreciate the unifying celebration of love amidst challenges. This universal theme has surpassed the constraints of language and region, connecting people through emotion and the desire for stories celebrating everlasting love.

The sustained interest in Cartland's works stems from their ability to provide escapism into a world where goodness prevails and love conquers all. Cartland's romantic idealism serves as an escape for readers seeking reassurance in an increasingly interconnected world with rapid technological development and social intricacies. This enduring fascination with her novels from readers in different cultural contexts highlights the unwavering demand for stories that celebrate human connections and emotional satisfaction.

In summary, Barbara Cartland's worldwide reach and influence demonstrate the continued affection for her romantic legacy. Her stories cross boundaries, changing understanding, nurturing compassion, and acting as a vehicle for universal realities. Through her literary works, Cartland has bestowed the world with stories that defy the confines of time and space whilst perpetuating an enduring legacy that affects future generations. Her romances, shaped by her global footprint, enduringly enrich human existence and demonstrate her status as an author transcending time, reason, romance, and compassion.

# Critiques and Counterpoints in Literature

As with any other prolific writer, literary criticism has always been inseparable from the discourse surrounding Barbara Cartland's works. While she was applauded for her ability to draw readers into a world of extravagant romance, there was also dissent regarding her writing and themes. Some critics charge that her books reinforce outdated views of gender relations and romance, offering a misguided and harmful perspective on love and relationships. Additionally, some scholars have taken issue with her storytelling devices and the lack of variety and depth in her character portrayals. Defenders of Cartland's work, however, insist that her unwavering devotion to romantic features has made the author popular with readers over the decades. They claim that this dedication to ideal love stories provides much-needed escape and relief to audiences overwhelmed by the pressures of everyday life. Furthermore, they cite the astonishing sales figures of her books as evidence of their enduring appeal, connecting readers to a timeless literary tradition. Some analysts have also described the importance of context in the perception of literature, noting that Cartland reflected the values and norms of society during her time.

From this viewpoint, it can be argued that although modern readers may find some elements of her stories to be outdated, they inform us in a profound way about how romantic literature has evolved throughout history. The arguments and counterarguments discussed in relation to Cartland's body of works highlight the ongoing debate regarding the significant role of romance literature in the construction of societal values and individual hopes and dreams, underscoring the weight of its influence.

## Preservation of Romantic Ideals

Romantic ideals remain at the roots of human civilisation- in literature, art, and culture. Cartland's life can best be described as one where she single-handedly fought to immortalise these romantic notions through her writing. Her numerous stories, with their expansive settings, transport readers to an enchanting world filled with chivalry, love, weddings, and more. This paradigm is only made possible through Cartland's heroes, who, in her novels, are selfless, honest, loyal, and devoted- the living proof of romantic ideals. Furthermore, these elements of heroism, sacrifice, kindness, and compassion intertwined with romantic relationships, which are ever-present in her works, demonstrate her understanding of her readers and society, thus preserving these elements within her works forever. These relationships illustrate during her lifetime that love is not merely a feeling but a bond anchored in respect and affection that endures the test of time. Such ideals put forth by revolutionary women like Cartland portray a world that will always need guidance and hope, even in changing eras when evoked, "love conquers all."

Moreover, Cartland's cultivation of a utopian vision of romance infuses her novels with a timeless quality, offering readers respite and encouragement in the uncompromising romanticism of her stories. After all, the maintenance of romantic values in Cartland's body of work stands as a source of hope, guiding countless generations to adopt the enduring ideals of love, compassion, and strength in their lives. This enduring influence, which transcends time and culture, sustains the idealistic essence of romance and cements her status as a foremost figure in romantic literature for future generations, making the audience feel the lasting impact of her stories.

## A Lasting Connection to Readers

Through words, her readers have 'bonded' with Barbara Cartland and her stories for countless years while maintaining awareness of her literary work. "The ability to arouse feelings and weave romance with her readers was a different level." This was Cartland's ability to forge bonds with an audience transcending beyond reading. The reasons behind her timeless appeal can be attributed to several aspects. First, a reader's faith in love is the guiding light. To accompany such love as a force, even Cartland put all her efforts into depicting love, trust, and positivity. Triumphing protagonists and the surge of love overcoming hurdles brought immense strength, enabling readers to believe in enduring hope even in the face of powerful adversity. This spirit strengthens the bond forged with readers.

Offering intricate, emotionally charged plots accompanied by compelling portrayals of love has created a phenomenon of passive empowerment among her readers, who become great participants. Alongside her characters, the 'romantic' Cartland enables her readers to experience refreshing emotions together.

Such qualities create an emotional bond with readers that remains in their hearts and minds long after they finish the book. Furthermore, the moral principles of chivalry, honour, and decorum, which Cartland unfailingly follows in her narratives, provide a path of morality that helps her readers navigate the intricacies of contemporary society. While nurturing a sense of moral clarity and ethical conviction among her readers, these values also encourage a shared connection. Lastly, the warmth Cartland extended to her audience in her interaction posters and addresses completes the bond between author and audience. Her engagement with the public not only sustains their appreciation of her but also fosters a sense of closeness, which cements their loyalty toward her work. Therefore, Cartland's boundless enlightenment to her readers transforms the relationship from mere admiration of literary artistry to an embrace of timeless affection that survives through the ages.

# Adapting Timeless Narratives to Modern Media

Although there have been global technological and cultural changes, Barbara Cartland's narratives continue to draw the attention of different audiences across age lines. Exploring new avenues of contemporary media requires considering how such captivating artworks can be presented to modern audiences.

Integrating her narratives into modern media presents the challenge of balancing the preservation of themes with the reinvention of elements. While honouring the creativity of her love stories, curators must also consider what today's world deems 'acceptable' and 'trendy.' This requires a fusion of past and present in a way that ensures the essence and magic of Cartland's stories remain intact in the world of modern mediums and multi-layered narratives of sophisticated fashion.

Incorporating visual and storyline frameworks that have come to define modern media is a crucial issue in this process. Cartland's tapestry of captivating worlds can be conveyed through film, television, or online platforms, each with its own opportunities and challenges. Elements such as clothing, scenery, and cameras must be woven into the plot in equal doses, subordinate to the sophisticated depth and emotional flow of Cartland's works.

Today's digital means of communication offer a new way to market Cartland's stories, allowing them to transcend the boundaries of literature and capture new audiences. With the launch of streaming services and digital publishing, these timeless stories can now be marketed to wider audiences, and more importantly, people from different parts of the world can easily access them. With carefully planned partnerships and marketing campaigns, Cartland's stories can be promoted to individuals far beyond the traditional readers' circle who now digitally reside in places where modern audiences go.

One of the most challenging tasks in retelling Cartland's stories for modern audiences is updating the depiction of relationships while retaining the essence of the original tale. Although developing new adaptations for them, creators need to respect the fundamental romantic elements of her literature, understand today's relationships and modify them in a way that resonates with many people. By achieving this balance, the transformed stories will not only capture the attention of viewers and readers but also allow them to experience a gentle yet strong embrace of familiarity and nostalgia.

Through adaptation, Cartland's prose no longer remains artifacts of the past; rather, modern media integrates them with renewed vigour. By leveraging the creative opportunities presented by new-age platforms, these narratives are now classic, further reinforcing their testament to love, passion, and enduring romance.

## Concluding Thoughts: An Enduring Legacy

For this reason, as we appraise Barbara Cartland's romantic legacy, it is apparent that her contributions embody much more than her novels. Having lasted for decades and written over a hundred books, Cartland's name will forever remain synonymous with romantic literature. It suffices to say that her narratives withstand the test of time and continue to cast a spell on readers worldwide.

Universal themes of love, honour, and devotion, which resonate with different cultures and endure throughout generations, keep Cartland's legacy alive. Cartland's contribution to literature lies in the fact that she created timeless stories that are still captivating today. Her masterful storytelling left a mark on readers when her works were published and continue to do so.

However, the core of her legacy and influence can also be seen in films, television, and even the digital world. Her literary works' adaptation into various forms of media displays their undying appeal to audiences. Not only does this enable new readers to discover her literary works, but it also brings forth opportunities to keep her legacy vibrant in contemporary society.

Admirers and critics alike realise that Cartland's legacy is undoubtedly marred with conflict. Many have argued that her literature promotes outdated depictions of how women and men should behave and conventional standards of love. While there is much criticism on this issue, one thing remains certain: her legacy firmly resides in the world of literature, and her influence is undoubtedly everlasting.

In summary, Barbara Cartland's lasting legacy is built upon admiration and respect carved in stone, as well as her everlasting narratives. She guides readers to realms filled with romance, chivalry, and timeless moral values and ensures that her legacy echoes into the distant days to come. With the progression of time in the literary world, Cartland's legacy serves as a testament to the myriad possibilities of romance literature and the captivating essence of love stories.

# Bibliographic Selection

## Some of Barbara Cartland's works

1. Cartland, B. (1925). *Jigsaw: An autobiography*. Hutchinson.
2. Cartland, B. (1931). *A virgin in paradise*. Farquharson.
3. Cartland, B. (1940). *The clipper romance*. Collins.
4. Cartland, B. (1941). *The sultana's dream*. Collins.
5. Cartland, B. (1944). *The army doctor's romance*. Collins.
6. Cartland, B. (1945). *A dream of love*. Collins.
7. Cartland, B. (1946). *The young contessa*. Collins.
8. Cartland, B. (1947). *The black raven*. Collins.
9. Cartland, B. (1948). *The flame is love*. Collins.
10. Cartland, B. (1949). *The moonlight Castle*. Collins.
11. Cartland, B. (1950). *The castle of love*. Collins.
12. Cartland, B. (1951). *The beloved rebel*. Collins.
13. Cartland, B. (1952). *The dark one*. Collins.
14. Cartland, B. (1953). *The devil in love*. Collins.
15. Cartland, B. (1954). *The dazzling diamond*. Collins.
16. Cartland, B. (1955). *The fugitive*. Collins.

17. Cartland, B. (1956). *The golden hawk*. Collins.
18. Cartland, B. (1957). *The guardian angel*. Collins.
19. Cartland, B. (1958). *The heart of gold*. Collins.
20. Cartland, B. (1959). *The heaven on earth*. Collins.
21. Cartland, B. (1960). *The palace of peril*. Collins.
22. Cartland, B. (1961). *The queen of love*. Collins.
23. Cartland, B. (1962). *The rainbow of love*. Collins.
24. Cartland, B. (1963). *The tender storm*. Collins.
25. Cartland, B. (1964). *The witch of the woods*. Collins.
26. Cartland, B. (1965). *A blade of grass*. Collins.
27. Cartland, B. (1966). *A danger to men*. Collins.
28. Cartland, B. (1967). *Love is the key*. Collins.
29. Cartland, B. (1968). *The night of the tempest*. Collins.
30. Cartland, B. (1969). *The prince in disguise*. Collins.
31. Cartland, B. (1970). *A ghost in Monte Carlo*. Collins.
32. Cartland, B. (1975). *Love is a stranger*. Collins.
33. Cartland, B. (1980). *Love is a wild bird*. Bantam Books.
34. Cartland, B. (1990). *The important night*. Fontana.
35. Cartland, B. (2000). *A dangerous infidelity*. Barbara Cartland.com.

# Books on the author

1. Adams, A. (1990). *Barbara Cartland: Her story*. Robson Books.

2. Allen, R. (1985). *The novels of Barbara Cartland: A reader's guide*. Frederick Muller.

3. Baker, L. (2001). *The romantic world of Barbara Cartland*. Parragon.

4. Barrow, R. (1995). *Barbara Cartland: The biography*. Pan Books.

5. Benson, R. (1988). *The Barbara Cartland phenomenon*. W.H. Allen.

6. Bradley, K. (2002). *Barbara Cartland: A critical biography*. McFarland.

7. Brooks, R. (1998). *The queen of romance: The life of Barbara Cartland*. Robson Books.

8. Carter, S. (2000). *Barbara Cartland and the romance novel*. Palgrave Macmillan.

9. Chapman, J. (1992). *The life and loves of Barbara Cartland*. Smith Gryphon.

10. Collins, M. (1997). *Barbara Cartland: Her life and times*. Orion.

11. Cook, R. (1987). *The romance of Barbara Cartland*. W.H. Allen.

12. Cooper, A. (2005). *Barbara Cartland: The unauthorized biography*. John Blake Publishing.

13. Davies, H. (1999). *The world of Barbara Cartland*. Parragon.

14. Edwards, L. (1994). *Barbara Cartland: A life of love*. Robson Books.

15. Fisher, M. (2003). *The enduring appeal of Barbara Cartland*. Virgin Books.

16. Foster, E. (1996). *The Barbara Cartland handbook*. Visible

Ink Press.

17. Gibson, R. (1989). *The romance and the reality: The life of Barbara Cartland*. W.H. Allen.

18. Green, J. (2004). *Barbara Cartland: The legend and the legacy*. John Wiley & Sons.

19. Harris, K. (1993). *The queen of romance: Barbara Cartland*. Smith Gryphon.

20. Hill, M. (1991). *The novels of Barbara Cartland: Themes and motifs*. Twayne Publishers.

21. James, P. (1986). *The Barbara Cartland story*. W.H. Allen.

22. Kelly, N. (2006). *Barbara Cartland: A life in pink*. John Blake Publishing.

23. King, B. (1998). *The romance revolution: Barbara Cartland and her influence*. Virgin Books.

24. Lane, S. (2002). *Barbara Cartland: The queen of clean romance*. Robson Books.

25. Lloyd, R. (1995). *The Barbara Cartland encyclopedia*. Visible Ink Press.

26. Mason, E. (1997). *The life and times of Barbara Cartland*. Orion.

27. Nelson, A. (2001). *Barbara Cartland: The romance and the reality*. Parragon.

28. Owen, M. (1999). *The world of Barbara Cartland: A pictorial biography*. Robson Books.

29. Parker, J. (1994). *The Barbara Cartland companion*. Smith Gryphon.

30. Quinn, R. (2003). *The queen of love: The life of Barbara Cartland*. John Wiley & Sons.

31. Reid, N. (1992). *The Barbara Cartland collection*. W.H.

Allen.

32. Scott, L. (1996). *The romance of Barbara Cartland: A critical study*. Twayne Publishers.

33. Taylor, K. (2000). *Barbara Cartland: The biography*. Orion.

34. Walker, R. (1993). *The novels of Barbara Cartland: A study guide*. Frederick Muller.

35. Young, E. (1995). *The Barbara Cartland scrapbook*. Robson Books.

# Various Sources

## Biographies and Life Studies

1. Johnson, L. M. (2023). *Barbara Cartland and the business of romance: Publishing strategies of a literary phenomenon*. Oxford University Press.

2. Williams, K. (2022). *The pink queen: Barbara Cartland's cultural impact on twentieth-century romance fiction*. Cambridge University Press.

3. Harris, E. D. (2021). Barbara Cartland's aristocratic fantasies:

Class performance and social aspiration in post-war Britain. *Journal of Popular Culture*, 54(3), 412-431. https://doi.org/10.1111/jpcu.12983

4. Thompson, S. (2020). *Beyond the pink: The literary life of Barbara Cartland*. Bloomsbury Academic.

5. Chen, M. (2021). Cartland's public persona: The creation and maintenance of the romance novelist as celebrity. *Celebrity Studies*, 12(1), 78-96. https://doi.org/10.1080/19392397.2020.1834538

6. Nelson, R. (2023). Barbara Cartland's humanitarian work: The overlooked legacy of a romance novelist. *Women's History Review*, 32(2), 209-227. https://doi.org/10.1080/09612025.2022.2065891

7. Parker, D. (2024). *The Cartland archives: New biographical insights from personal papers*. Routledge.

## Literary Analysis and Criticism

8. Roberts, A. (2022). Formula and innovation: Narrative structures in Barbara Cartland's romance fiction. *Journal of Popular Romance Studies*, 11(1), 45-67. https://doi.org/10.2964/jprs.v11i1.124

9. Zhang, Y. (2023). Virginity and virtue: Sexual politics in Barbara Cartland's historical romances. *Feminist Media Studies*, 23(4), 527-544. https://doi.org/10.1080/14680777.2022.2103458

10. Greenfield, L. K. (2021). Cartland's heroines: Evolving representations of femininity across seven decades. *Literature Compass*, 18(3), e12598. https://doi.org/10.1111/lic3.12598

11. Alvarez, M. (2020). The persistent aristocracy: Class structures in Barbara Cartland's historical fiction. *Journal of Class Studies*, 7(2), 183-201. https://doi.org/10.1080/2158037X.2020.1732584

12. Peterson, T. H. (2024). Cartland's medievalism: Historical accuracy and romantic imagination in her historical novels. *Studies in Medievalism*, 33(1), 78-96. https://doi.org/10.1353/stm.2024.0005

13. Wilson, C. R. (2022). Barbara Cartland and the evolution of romance publishing, 1925-2000. *Book History*, 25(1), 312-338. https://doi.org/10.1353/bh.2022.0011

14. Kumar, P. (2023). Orientalism and exoticism in Barbara Cartland's international romances. *Postcolonial Studies*, 26(2), 217-235. https://doi.org/10.1080/13688790.2022.2149765

## Cultural Impact and Reception

15. Radway, J. A., & Martinez, E. (2021). Cartland readers: Reception studies and the consumption of romance fiction in post-war Britain. *European Journal of Cultural Studies*, 24(3), 542-561. https://doi.org/10.1177/13675494211001568

16. Thomas, B. (2020). Barbara Cartland and the popular romance market: Influence on genre conventions and publishing trends. *Publishing Research Quarterly*, 36(4), 579-597. https://doi.org/10.1007/s12109-020-09741-1

17. Frost, D. (2022). Pink packaging and marketing strategies: The visual branding of Barbara Cartland novels. *Journal of Visual Culture*, 21(1), 88-107. https://doi.org/10.1177/14704129211067325

18. Langford, H. (2023). The Cartland effect: Cultural perceptions of romance fiction in the late twentieth century. *Cultural Studies*, 37(1), 124-142. https://doi.org/10.1080/09502386.2022.2083867

19. O'Brien, K. (2024). Barbara Cartland and the media: Television appearances and public persona construction. *Media, Culture & Society*, 46(2), 319-337. https://doi.org/10.1177/01634437231587429

20. Ahmed, S. (2023). Romance novel covers: The visual evolution of Barbara Cartland's book design. *Journal of Design History*, 36(1), 67-85. https://doi.org/10.1093/jdh/epac032

## Historical and Contextual Studies

21. Harrison, P. (2021). Barbara Cartland and the aristocratic revival in post-war British popular culture. *Contemporary British History*, 35(3), 428-446. https://doi.org/10.1080/13619462.2021.1901651

22. Miller, J. (2022). Romance in recession: Barbara Cartland's publishing success during economic downturns. *Business History*, 64(8), 1245-1264. https://doi.org/10.1080/00076791.2021.1969935

23. Watkins, S. (2023). Barbara Cartland and the British social landscape, 1945-1990: Romance as cultural barometer. *Journal of British Studies*, 62(2), 371-392. https://doi.org/10.1017/jbr.2022.159

24. Franklin, C. (2021). Romance fiction during wartime: Barbara Cartland's early career and literary responses to conflict. *Literature and History*, 30(1), 76-94. https://doi.org/10.1177/03061973211000235

25. Donovan, P. (2024). *From aristocracy to mass market: Barbara Cartland and the democratization of romance*. Manchester University Press.

## Comparative Studies and Literary Relationships

26. Richardson, A. (2022). Barbara Cartland and Georgette Heyer: Competing visions of historical romance. *Neo-Victorian Studies*, 15(1), 152-176. https://doi.org/10.5281/zenodo.6513942

27. Powell, M. (2023). Beyond bodice-rippers: Barbara Cartland, Mills & Boon, and the evolution of romance publishing houses. *Journal of Publishing Culture*, 10(2), 213-231. https://doi.org/10.1080/21670811.2022.2118475

28. Lee, J. (2021). From Cartland to contemporary: Tracing the lineage of modern romance fiction. *Genre*, 54(1), 61-88. https://doi.org/10.1215/00166928-8911425

29. Benstock, S., & Ferris, T. (2024). Barbara Cartland and her literary descendants: Influence on contemporary romance authors. *Women's Writing*, 31(1), 83-102. https://doi.org/10.1080/09699082.2023.2176543

## Legacy and Digital Afterlife

30. Young, K. (2023). Barbara Cartland in the digital age: The afterlife of her novels in e-publishing and audiobooks. *Convergence: The International Journal of Research into New Media Technologies*, 29(1), 115-133. https://doi.org/10.1177/13548565221139647

31. Reynolds, M. (2024). The Cartland adaptation: Screen versions of Barbara Cartland's novels from 1980 to present. *Adaptation: The Journal of Literature on Screen Studies*, 17(1), 42-61. https://doi.org/10.1093/adaptation/apac012

32. Gordon, S. (2022). Barbara Cartland's enduring brand: Literary estates and author legacies in popular fiction. *LOGOS: Journal of the World Publishing Community*, 33(2), 12-29. https://doi.org/10.1163/18784712-20221234

33. Brennan, J. (2023). Barbara Cartland and twenty-first century romance: Continuities and disruptions in the genre. *Popular Culture Studies Journal*, 11(1), 78-96. https://doi.org/10.15340/2148937611.1.5

34. Wu, L. (2022). Digital preservation of Barbara Cartland's literary corpus: Challenges and opportunities. *Digital Scholarship in the Humanities*, 37(3), 728-745. https://doi.org/10.109

3/llc/fqab098

35. Turner, E. (2024). Reappraising Barbara Cartland: Academic legitimation of a popular romance novelist. *Journal of Literary Studies*, 40(1), 53-72. https://doi.org/10.1080/02564718.2023.2267891

www.ingramcontent.com/pod-product-compliance
Lightning Source LLC
Chambersburg PA
CBHW071236070526
44583CB00017B/2206